BETTY FRIEDAN

Fighter for Women's Rights

Sondra Henry and Emily Taitz

—Contemporary Women Series—

ENSLOW PUBLISHERS, INC.

Bloy St. & Ramsey Ave.   P.O. Box 38
Box 777   Aldershot
Hillside, NJ 07205   Hants GU12 6BP
U.S.A.   U.K.

J 305.42092 F899h 1990
Henry, Sondra.
Betty Friedan, fighter for
 women's rights MAR 14 '12

Copyright © 1990 by Sondra Henry and Emily Taitz

All rights reserved.

No part of this book may be reproduced by any means
without the written permission of the publisher.

Library of Congress Cataloging-in-Publication Data

Henry, Sondra.
 Betty Friedan, fighter for women's rights / by Sondra Henry
and Emily Taitz.
  p. cm. — (Contemporary women series)
 Summary: A biography of the author of "The Feminine Mystique"
and founder of the National Organization for Women.
 ISBN 0-89490-292-X
 1. Friedan, Betty — Juvenile literature. 2. Feminists —
United States — Biography — Juvenile literature. [1. Friedan,
Betty. 2. Feminists.] I. Taitz, Emily. II. Title. III. Series.
HQ1413.F75H46   1990
305.42'092 — dc20
[B]
[92]   89-23582
                                         CIP
                                         AC

Printed in the United States of America

10 9 8 7 6 5 4 3 2 1

Illustration Credits:
Courtesy LILITH, the Jewish women's magazine, p. 12;
Copyright © Stephenie Hollyman, p. 7; Smith College
Archives, Smith College, pp. 24, 28, 116; The Schlesinger
Library, Radcliffe College, pp. 18, 32, 36, 41, 46, 55, 61,
66, 71, 75, 79, 86, 92, 95, 97, 103, 105, 111.

Cover Photo: © 1985 Susan Wood.

Contents

Acknowledgments

We would like to thank the following people for their help in researching Betty Friedan's life.

All the librarians at the Schlesinger Library at Radcliffe College, Smith College Archives, and the Peoria Public Library.

Christopher Davidson, Robert Elliott, Robert Fields, Tamar Taitz Fields, Elizabeth Friedman, Rabbi Laura Geller, Doris Gold, Harry Goldstein, Dr. Edward Henry, Gordon M. Henry, Stephenie Hollyman, Helene Lipkin, Harriet Vance Parkhurst, Dr. John Parkhurst, Letty Cottin Pogrebin, Patricia Henry Sachs, Susan Weidman Schneider and *Lilith* magazine, Amy Stone, Marian Sprenger, Joan Swirsky, Alan Walker, Nancy Goldstein Zwicky.

1

From Peoria to Nairobi

Under the shade of a large tree, a woman sits crosslegged on the ground, listening and talking. The tree is on the campus of Nairobi University, in Kenya, far away from the American Midwest where she was born and raised.

The woman, Betty Friedan, is short and slightly plump. She has heavy-lidded eyes under dark eyebrows, a long prominent nose, and a firm mouth. A thick head of gray hair frames her face. Betty could easily pass for someone's grandmother, as indeed she is.

Here in Kenya she is surrounded by women from dozens of different countries. The Africans are dressed in the colorful print garments of their native lands. The Muslim women from Iran are covered with black veils called chadors. Still others wear saris — the Indian wraparound dresses — Asian trousers, or Western-style cottons. The women represent many shades of color and many more shades of opinion.

Betty Friedan is listening to a woman whom she calls Sister Sara. Sara describes her hard life as a farmer in rural Kenya. On an average day she must walk long distances, barefoot, to fetch water. She returns to her home carrying a large clay pot balanced on her head. Sara must also shop, carry wood for the fire, feed the family, take care of the children and the cattle.

Betty is indignant as she begins to understand Sara's difficult life. "Women are the professors of life," Betty Friedan tells those assembled around her. "We earn our degrees from the theater of life."

It is July 1985. Here in Kenya, Betty is attending Forum '85, a series of seminars and workshops involving 11,000 women. The women represent nongovernmental organizations in countries throughout the world. They have come together to share their experience and knowledge.

Forum '85 is occurring at the same time and place as the formal U.N.-sponsored Decade of Women conference. Previous U.N. women's conferences in Mexico City and in Copenhagen, Denmark, were held in 1975 and 1980. This third one marks a continuing progress for some women. For others it is an important first breakthrough.

In Mexico City and Copenhagen the women were mainly the wives of political leaders and were not really concerned with women's rights. In Nairobi the delegates are more independent, and many are strong believers in women's rights.

Betty had attended both of the other conferences too. She had been shocked and angry at how politics had been used to prevent any real accomplishments at those meetings. She had also been appalled by the open hatred of Jews and Israel (anti-Semitism) that had surfaced there. This time, things promised to be different.

"There is no provision for permanent machinery at the U.N. for monitoring women's progress, so we've got to see that something real is accomplished," said Betty shortly before the conference began.

Betty is the head of the unofficial delegation from NOW, the National Organization for Women. She requested in advance "a tree with shade for twenty people," explaining: "I plan to sit under it every day and talk about the future of feminism."

The Bible tells the story of Deborah, a heroine and a judge in

6

ancient Israel. Deborah, too, sat under the shade of a tree. She advised her people and prophesied about the future.

Betty is living more than two thousand years after Deborah. Yet the two women do have a few things in common. Both were strong and wise and operated in a world where most leaders were men. Both became honored and respected in their own time.

Deborah led an army into battle. Her victory made history and changed the lives of many people in the ancient Middle East.

Betty led the women of America into a different kind of battle, the

Betty Friedan sat under a tree discussing women's issues at the Nairobi women's conference.

battle for equal rights and equal opportunities. This ongoing struggle also has made history. In addition it has changed the lives of women, men, and children in her own country and throughout the world.

Betty Friedan is especially familiar with the remarkable changes that have affected Western women in her lifetime. A great many of these changes are due to her own work, commitment, and fiery dedication.

At the conference in Nairobi, Betty Friedan is again being interviewed. She comments that American women are now suffering a backlash to the women's movement. The young women of today, she says, do not know how long and hard a road has been traveled in the last twenty-five years.

It is incredible, Betty told the reporter. All the rights and changed attitudes were barely achieved before they were forgotten. Betty believes that people ought to know the way it was.

It took Betty Naomi Goldstein Friedan more than sixty years to travel to this worldwide gathering of women in Nairobi. Her journey began with a lonely, and sometimes difficult childhood in Peoria, Illinois. From there, Betty became a serious student, then a committed researcher, an accomplished author, and a tireless organizer.

In her later years she was famous as both a media personality and the subject of thousands of jokes. She is an international speaker and an adviser to presidents. In her personal life, Betty was a wife and a loving mother. Today she is a proud grandmother.

Some people are quick to call her an enemy, but more consider her a good and loyal friend. Through it all—the fame, the disappointments, and the successes—this women's rights leader can still remember herself as the lonely young girl who once proclaimed: "If they don't like me, they will learn to respect me."

2

"I Want My Life To Be Full of Beauty"

It was hard growing up. She needed braces on her teeth and glasses for her weak eyes. Few people would ever have said that Bettye Naomi Goldstein was pretty.

Bettye (who would later drop the *e* at the end of her name) certainly did not resemble the ideal little girl of her time, one with blond curls, a pert nose, and dimples. Instead, she had a long nose and thick, wiry, dark hair that resisted most attempts to keep it in place. In a world where being pretty was considered important, Betty soon realized that if she wanted praise or admiration, she would have to find other ways to get it.

Born on February 4, 1921, Betty was the first child of Miriam and Harry Goldstein. From the day she was born, she was not a healthy baby. Dr. Cooley, who delivered her at Proctor Hospital in Peoria, advised her parents that her legs would probably straighten out. Of course, he explained, she would have to wear braces for a few years.

Harry Goldstein, Betty's father, had journeyed to the United States from Eastern Europe in the early part of the twentieth century. He was still young then and had arrived together with his family. Settled in St. Louis, Missouri, the family struggled to earn a living and build a new life. Harry had no time or money for an education. He had helped to support his family since he was a child and was used to hard work.

Like many Jewish immigrants before him, Harry began his career as a peddler. Leaving St. Louis, he traveled north into Illinois.

When Harry first came to Peoria it was a thriving city of 100,000 people. Grain from Midwestern wheat fields and meat from Chicago were sent to Peoria's factories to be processed and forwarded to stores throughout the country. Plants manufactured distilled whiskey and tractors. Peoria seemed like a good place to settle.

Harry Goldstein came with a small supply of buttons that he sold from street corners in his adopted city. But it was not long before he had saved enough for a small store. From buttons he progressed to more expensive goods and soon had a prosperous jewelry business selling watches, fine china, silver, and diamonds.

Harry was attracted to young, good-looking Miriam Horwitz who seemed to be everything he wanted in a wife. Miriam fell in love with Harry too. However, her parents disapproved of the match. Harry was not well educated, whereas Miriam had graduated from Peoria's Bradley College and was the daughter of a prominent local doctor. In addition Harry was eighteen years older than Miriam. Miriam was sent out of town in the hope that she would forget Harry Goldstein. But she was determined to marry him.

When Miriam and Harry married in 1920, he was already forty years old and a successful businessman. Miriam, only twenty-two, had been working for a local newspaper. Shortly after she married, she became pregnant and stopped work. In those days it was considered unusual for a married woman to work and totally improper if she was expecting a baby.

Nine months later, Betty Naomi was born. Another daughter, Amy, was born shortly after, and then a son, Harry. The other children seemed much easier to care for after Betty.

Miriam Goldstein felt that her oldest child picked up every cold or flu germ that passed through Peoria. As Betty grew older, she often wheezed and coughed through the winters.

Struggling to stay healthy was a difficult job. Eventually the heavy braces came off Betty's legs, but she was never much good at sports. She grew to love hiking but not the dancing lessons her mother arranged.

When she was old enough for school, Betty's life became more interesting. Reading, writing, and arithmetic were easy for her, and she quickly impressed her teachers at the Whittier grade school. She had learned to read so quickly that from first grade she was moved up to second, then skipped again from fourth to fifth grade.

Books became Betty's passion, and she could never get enough to read. She dreamed that when she grew up she would be a librarian. That way, she reasoned, she would always be among books.

When she wasn't reading, Betty loved dressing up in mother's old clothes. In her pretend games, Betty could be anyone she wanted. Alone in her room, or with playmates, she would let her imagination roam far away from the red brick house on Farmington Road where she lived. Inside her head she had all sorts of adventures. She made up plays in which she was the beautiful heroine she could not be in real life.

From the outside it might have been difficult to guess that Betty Goldstein was ever discontented. Her home was gracious and well cared for. Across the street, Betty and her sister, Amy, could play in their favorite grove of trees in Bradley Park. Here she and Amy walked each morning together with their father before he went off to his long day of work in the store.

Betty made friends in school and often spent her free time playing with Nancy, Otty, and Marian. Sometimes a few boys joined them too. Although her friends teased her and called her "bookworm" because she loved to read so much, they liked her for herself and did not judge her for the way she looked.

Even when she was very young, Betty was good at organizing

When she was old enough for school, Betty quickly impressed her teachers.

clubs. The first was the Gummy-Gummy Club, a group of children who agreed to chew gum together, sometimes in the classroom, where it was strictly forbidden. Then there were the Detective Club, and the Baddy-Baddy Club.

As the ringleader of the Baddy-Baddy Club, Betty encouraged its members to be disruptive in class, making coughing noises or "accidently" dropping books on the floor.

When the school principal found out about the Baddy-Baddies, he called Betty into his office to reprimand her.

"You have a talent for leadership," the principal said. He strongly suggested that she use her talent in more constructive ways.

After school, parents like Betty's, who could afford it, arranged activities for their children. Of course there were school teams, but Betty never cared for sports. At that time, sports were considered to be for boys. Girls were not encouraged to participate if they did not want to.

For girls, dancing lessons were the most popular, but not for Betty. She felt awkward and knew she was not graceful.

Her mother looked around for something else and decided to enroll her in dramatic school. Dramatics turned out to be just the thing for Betty. She had a chance to read plays, to write her own, and of course to act in them. Occasionally, theater groups came through Peoria and she would go to see a play.

Yet, in spite of a life that seemed so perfect on the outside, Betty was lonely and often angry. Frequently she directed her quick temper against her brother and sister. She shouted at them and sometimes threw things when her anger got the best of her. In a college essay about herself, Betty wrote that "when she was five she hit a boy over the head with a hoe," and at ten, "she tore a handful of hair out of a girl's head."

Betty felt that her mother was always nagging her and was never satisfied. Knowing that Miriam scolded everyone in the family, even her father, did not make it less painful for Betty to accept. She was too

13

young to understand that this was her mother's way of dealing with problems she could not solve.

Miriam too seemed to have a happy life on the outside. She was a good-looking woman who could afford fine clothes and looked well in them. She had a beautiful home and a comfortable life. Golf and horseback riding were among her accomplishments. Harry provided well for her and their children.

Still, Miriam Goldstein felt dissatisfied. Betty later wrote in her book *The Second Stage* that although her mother "ran the Sunday School one year, the Community Chest the next, played endless games of bridge and mah-jongg," it was not enough for her boundless energies.

Betty's mother believed she was "above" her husband Harry in education and in social status. When she was twenty-two, Miriam had insisted on marrying Harry. Ten years later she was disappointed with her husband and resented having to depend on him for an allowance.

With the Great Depression in the 1930s came a lack of jobs and money in the United States. It began to affect the Goldstein's jewelry business, and things got worse for Miriam as the family had less money to spend. Now they had to let the maid and chauffeur go and manage without that extra help.

During those years Miriam found it harder to cope with reality. Betty recalled her mother "hiding the bills she charged, secretly trying her hand at gambling...and losing more, until she had to confess; causing terrible battles that shook our house at night."

Hearing her parents shouting at each other made Betty feel frightened and miserable. From behind the door of her room, she tried not to listen to the furious anger of her father when he found out about her mother's gambling debts.

Despite all this, Betty remembers her father at that time as "a genial man." "He loved his family and his home and his friends and his business," wrote Betty. "Everyone greeted him by name when he walked down the business section of Peoria."

Betty graduated from grade school and entered Roosevelt Junior High. She was praised by her teachers for her high marks and brought home report cards filled mostly with As. In addition, there were school activities, attendance at Roosevelt Junior High's basketball games, and get-togethers with friends.

Betty also wrote for the junior high school newspaper, *The Reflector*. It was satisfying to see her name in print and know that her friends and classmates were reading the words she had written.

Betty's brother, Harry, thought his sister was extremely popular. Five years younger than Betty, Harry still remembers the many meetings and parties Betty had at their home. He recalled that her friends used to offer him a nickel so that he would go away and not bother them.

But for all its busyness, junior high school was a time for change. These changes, although not always discussed, were more important than grades or school newspapers or class plays. The girls, especially, were changing and growing into young women.

The carefree days at Whittier Grade School and Roosevelt Junior High, when Betty played kissing games like Post Office or Hide-in-the-Dark on Friday nights, were over. In Central High, students were divided up into social clubs called fraternities and sororities. Because of old prejudices against Jews, Jewish boys and girls were excluded from these groups.

Until then it hadn't mattered that Betty was Jewish. But when it came time to be invited into a sorority, Betty was the only girl in her class left off the list. She alone would not be included in the comfortable world of Friday-night socials, dances, and double dates.

How painful it was for Betty the day she found out! It didn't help when her father explained to her that grown-up Jews and gentiles did not mix in Peoria either. Her father had often told her that "the people friendly to him in business would not speak to him after sundown." That was when business was over and socializing began. Nor could Jews join the country club, no matter how rich they were.

It didn't make Betty feel better to pretend she didn't care. She cared desperately.

And now, as if it wasn't bad enough being Jewish in a town that looked down on Jews, Betty's looks became more important too. Rude boys made unpleasant comments about her, and Betty felt more self-conscious than ever.

The boy friends of her early school years — Ned, Jimmy, Bob, and Billy — were strangers now. They chose the pretty, Christian girls to take to movies and school dances. On the rare occasions when Betty did have a date, she was sure that the boys were "rejects" and "misfits just like me."

Betty still recalls lonely days sitting in an abandoned cemetery near her home, her eyes filled with tears.

Feeling sorry for herself, however, did not make Betty happier. It only made things worse at home. Although her mother felt bad for Betty, it seemed that she only nagged her more, offering all kinds of useless advice.

Being a good student did not solve Betty's problems, either. In the 1930s and '40s many people believed that it was not wise for a girl to be too smart. It scared off the boys and would never make her popular. Popular seemed the most important thing to be, and Betty sometimes even made believe she wasn't so bright, in hopes that it would help her make more friends. Nothing changed.

Escape into books was one way to forget the miseries of being a teenager who didn't fit in anywhere. Every minute with a book was one less minute in the painful world of reality. Betty's father actually forbid her to take out more than five books at a time from the library. He felt that her life should be more balanced.

Besides using books as an escape, Betty loved literature. An English teacher, Miss Crowder, had introduced her to poetry and essays as well as fiction. Betty spent long hours reading the work of Emily Dickinson, one of her favorite poets.

She also began writing book reviews for the Central High paper under a heading titled "Opinions." Soon she had her own column, "Cabbages and Kings," in which she could write about whatever she pleased.

Writing for the school newspaper was one of the few things that pleased her mother too. Miriam had loved being Woman's Page editor of the Peoria newspaper. In most areas, Betty believed, Miriam was disappointed in her and wished she was someone else. But Miriam was proud of Betty's writing.

Slowly, the pain of social rejection lessened, and Betty learned to compensate with other activities. She joined clubs, entered essay contests, acted in school plays, and worked hard in her classes. The subjects she chose to study were the most difficult in the school. She took English, French, algebra, Latin, and chemistry.

It was chemistry she loved best and in which she excelled above the other subjects. She read about Madame Marie Curie, the French scientist who discovered radium and who had received two Nobel prizes for her work. How Betty wished she could do something like that! But teachers discouraged her. In the 1930s, girls were not encouraged to study science. They were advised to become nurses, secretaries, or lab technicians.

In her senior year at high school, Betty tried to brush aside her problems and bury herself in work and activities. Inside she felt shy and almost feared making new friends. Her close friends from those years — Harriet Vance, John Parkhurst, Paul Jordan, Doug Palmer, and a few others — find it hard to believe that Betty was unhappy and lonely in high school.

"Why, she was involved in every activity there was," John (called Parky by his friends) insisted. "She was well known and popular."

"We were together on the school newspaper and on the high school speech team, and were both public speakers," says Parky. He still recalls proudly the Memorial Day service in 1937 in Peoria's Court-

17

Betty's mother, Miriam, had loved being an editor of the Peoria newspaper and was proud of Betty's writing.

house Square. He and Betty read excerpts from famous speeches in front of the whole town.

Both Harriet and John remember the parties Betty had at her home throughout her high school years. "Great big parties, where all the kids who were anybody came, and we had a wonderful time!"

Harriet does understand some of Betty's unhappiness. Thinking back on those times, she explains: "A man could be happy if he was just busy with activities. A girl can begin to brood if she doesn't have many dates."

In her senior year Betty, together with Paul Jordan, Doug Palmer, and John Parkhurst, organized *Tide*, Central High's literary magazine. The group raised money, ran editorial meetings, proofread articles, and put together each issue. When *Tide* was a success, they were proud and happy. Betty would remember this as one of the big achievements of her high school years.

Another memory that was special was when she won the dramatic award. The prize was given to her for her part as the mad wife in the dramatized version of the novel *Jane Eyre* by Charlotte Bronte. Although it was a small part, Betty acted so well that she was the hit of the show.

Her writing talent gave her other chances to shine. She won an essay contest on "Why I Am Proud to be an American."

At seventeen, Betty was beginning, slowly, to feel a little better about herself. Although she never really got over what she considered the hurt of rejection by her classmates, she learned to make up for it in other ways. However, she still longed for the things she did not have. At night, she prayed for "a work of my own to do, and a boy who would love me best."

In an essay written during her seventeenth year, Betty's longings and hopes are clearly expressed. "I want my life to be full of beauty, and I want to create beauty. I want to fall in love and be loved and be needed by someone. I want to have children..."

Betty was among the five valedictorians—the five highest

achievers of the graduating class of June, 1938. She had been accepted into Smith, one of the finest women's colleges in the country.

That fall, she and her friend Harriet boarded a train and left Peoria for the long trip to college. Betty was eager, excited, and determined to make something of herself. However, she had not forgiven Central High's students for their rejection, and vowed that she would never return to Peoria.

3

Off to College at Last

There was a soft beauty to Smith College that was very different from the flat Midwestern prairie land where Betty had grown up. Here, there were rolling green hills, colonial brick buildings covered with ivy, and clumps of birch trees. Picturesque Paradise Lake was tucked away into a corner of the campus and helped to create a feeling of serenity and coziness. Nearby, the town of Northampton completed the picture of a typical New England countryside.

It was easy to be a student at Smith, to spend hours in the library reading or writing, to sit on the lawn and have long discussions about life and love with friends.

Now was the time to explore ideas and experience new things. One of these ideas was the feeling of identification Betty had as a Jew.

Betty remembered fondly the family seders, the ritual dinners at the Passover holiday, and going to temple on the Jewish New Year. However, she always felt that being Jewish in Peoria had kept her mother from membership in the country club — something she thought Miriam had wanted very badly. It had prevented Betty from being accepted in a high school sorority.

Betty remembered speaking to the rabbi of Temple Anshei Emet just before her confirmation, the ceremony at which young people affirmed their belief in their religion. She had been chosen as the student who would present flowers to the temple on behalf of the confirmation class. The idea worried her.

"Rabbi," she said hesitatingly, "I don't think I believe in God."

"Keep it to yourself," the rabbi answered, trying to reassure her.

He may have understood that, as a young person, Betty would have many questions about faith and assumed that her doubts would pass. From Betty's viewpoint, however, the rabbi had failed her when she needed help, and being confirmed did not make her feel more secure or happy about Judaism.

Now at Smith, she began to see her Jewish identity differently. As a freshman, Betty met with anti-Semitism from both Christians and Jews. Betty defined an anti-Semitic Jew as a Jewish person who didn't like being Jewish and didn't want to identify with other Jews. She was especially struck by a few Jewish girls who lived in her dorm, Chapin House.

It was shortly before World War II, and the college circulated a petition urging President Roosevelt to allow Jewish immigrants to come to America. Jews were being persecuted and killed in Europe and desperately needed a safe place to live. To Betty's amazement, these girls refused to support the resolution to help other Jews, even though many of their Christian classmates did.

Betty's sense of justice, a trait that would remain with her throughout her life, brought her to sign that petition as it lay on the hall table in her dorm. She waited to see if the other Jewish girls would do the same. They never did.

Later in her college career, when Betty helped to organize a literary magazine for Smith, her first story would be called "The Scapegoat." It told about a Jewish girl who was rejected by all the girls in her dorm—Jews as well as non-Jews. Since everyone else had turned against her, the Jewish girls did too. This was Betty's way of expressing her ideas about the anti-Semitic Jew.

But besides studies and serious ideas, there were good times too. In her sophomore year at Smith, Betty was honored with an appointment to the Sophomore Push Committee. This was the highest honor a second-year student could achieve. The thirty-five young women on the committee served as ushers and pages at the annual graduation. They also helped to decorate the gymnasium for senior festivities, served a special lunch to the senior class, and made sure that everything ran smoothly.

The title Push Committee came from one of the functions of those sophomore students during the precommencement period. On a specific day, the seniors rolled giant rings, called hoops, along the ground. The girl whose hoop remained upright, and who finished first, was the winner. On hoop-rolling day, committee members *pushed back* the spectators who crowded around to watch the festivities and cheer on their friends.

In a yearbook picture of those thirty-five sophomores, Betty is somewhere in the middle. Like her classmates, she is dressed in a long evening gown. Her dark hair is softly waved and touching her shoulders. She is five-feet-two, slim, and well-dressed.

At Smith, Betty Goldstein shared activities, work, and feelings with her friends. She was well-liked and respected on campus by both students and teachers.

In Smith's yearbook Betty's picture appears many times. She is usually dressed in a skirt, a white blouse under a crew-neck sweater, "bobby" socks (ankle-length white socks), and saddle shoes. Her dark, solemn eyes look out under heavy eyebrows, and her lips are accented by the bright red lipstick that was the fashion during those years.

A psychology major, Betty studied with Dr. Kurt Koffka. He was a German psychologist who became famous for his theory that things must be understood as a whole, not just by analyzing their parts.

Betty was the favorite of the psychology department and a member of the Psychology Club. She was elected to the two honor societies on campus. These are reserved for students who receive top grades in their classes.

School life was perfect, or so it seemed. But just like her childhood back home in Peoria, this picture too had hidden flaws.

Betty still often felt homely and left out. When her friends went out with boys, she remained behind with her work. There was only an occasional date, arranged for her by a girlfriend.

Betty longed for a real boyfriend of her own. Her friend Harriet

In 1942, Betty (standing second from right in second row) was an honor student at Smith College.

was practically engaged to John Parkhurst, her high school sweetheart. So many other students had boyfriends, became engaged, and married.

Having someone that "loved her best" was an old dream that she had prayed for all through her high school years. However, during her years at Smith, Betty never would feel enough security to develop a relationship with a boy, even when there was a chance to do so.

Although Betty always felt insecure within herself, other people never saw her that way. In her sophomore year Betty remembers that during a class discussion a professor said to her: "Miss Goldstein, you lack humility. You are too arrogant, you lack humility!"

Betty did act very sure of herself. Repeating her success in high school, she again organized a literary magazine, this time with classmate Mary Anne Guitar and a few other girls. She edited stories and wrote her own. Choosing from a variety of poems and essays written by fellow students, Betty planned each issue with much thought.

Back in Peoria, relations with her parents remained a problem. People in the community saw Betty's mother as beautiful and accomplished. But Betty and her sister, Amy, felt that she was overcritical. Much later, Amy would recall that their mother made each of them feel that they had disappointed her. "I was the pretty one...She was ugly and I was dumb," she said bitterly. Amy knew that it wasn't true, but their mother's attitude had fueled the rivalry between the two sisters.

There were problems with her father too. Betty knew that Harry adored and admired her for her brilliance in school and for her writing ability. He even guarded the poems she wrote in his safe-deposit box and openly bragged about her accomplishments to friends and customers. Harry often sought her out to speak with her, both in her high school and college years. But Betty would remember how often she had turned away from him and how much her mother's criticism of him distressed her.

When her father became sick and had to give over the business to

25

her mother, Miriam was happier. Forced to take on the running of the Goldstein jewelry store, the digestive ailments that had plagued her for many years went away. Always active in different causes, she now devoted her considerable energies to the family business.

This change in Miriam seemed to offer a respite to family members. However, the groundwork of disapproval she had laid would remain with Betty and her sister throughout their youth and into their adult years.

In the spring of her junior year, Betty tried out for *SCAN*, the college newspaper. This was a tense time for her.

That same week, Betty began coughing and couldn't stop. At first it seemed like nothing more than another familiar bout of bronchitis. But soon she began to feel breathless, and her friends quickly took her to the infirmary.

Asthma was the doctor's explanation. She had had an asthma attack. That led to a collapsed lung. It was serious enough for Betty to be hospitalized and for her mother to come from Peoria and help take care of her.

Asthma is frequently an allergic reaction that makes it difficult to breath. It usually becomes worse when you are upset, the doctor explained. This was the beginning of a problem that would often return to plague Betty Goldstein.

Despite that scare, however, the rest of Betty's college career was relatively healthy. Being "big woman on campus" was a role Betty enjoyed and on which she thrived. Teachers and students admired her.

Betty also spent summers doing things she liked best: a temporary job at the Peoria newspaper, summer courses, discussing and debating and, of course, writing.

One vacation, the summer of 1941, she would long remember as the most perfect of all. It was spent in Monteagle, Tennessee at a place called the Highlander Folk School. Described as a "labor school in the mountains of Tennessee," it was a place where members of trade unions came to learn about labor law and union organizing. They also held a summer writer's workshop that Betty attended.

In an essay entitled *"Learning the Score,"* which she wrote at the Highlander Folk School, Betty penned the following words:

"I began to understand that the things you were told were devices to keep you from thinking."

It was ideas such as this that laid the groundwork for Betty's own philosophy in *The Feminine Mystique* — a book that changed the world. Much later in her life, Betty would find that the Highlander Folk School was looked at with suspicion by the FBI.

More quickly than she could have imagined, four years of college were over. It was 1942, and Betty was graduating. This year it was she who was participating in hoop-rolling contests while the sophomore committee girls were pushing back enthusiastic crowds.

Now it was Betty and her friends being served at the senior class luncheon by the sophomore honorees. And then at last she was marching down the aisle at graduation.

"Bettye Naomi Goldstein."

Her name was one of four who received recognition as *summa cum laude,* "with highest praise."

"Bettye Naomi Goldstein."

Elected to academic honor societies *Phi Beta Kappa* and *Sigma Xi.*

"Bettye Naomi Goldstein."

Again she was singled out with a much-coveted fellowship to do graduate work in psychology at the University of California at Berkeley.

It was all so exciting and impressive. It almost made her forget the fear she had buried deep inside her. In spite of all the awards, Betty was frightened about leading an adult, independent life.

Not until years later was Betty able to admit all her insecurities about herself. And it was still later before she could bring herself to

27

Betty graduated from Smith as one of the top four students in her class.

write about the disappointment and anger she felt when her father did not come to her graduation.

Harry Goldstein Sr. had suffered for several years from high blood pressure and heart problems. He pleaded illness at graduation time. Later he admitted that he thought Betty would have been ashamed of him.

His absence took some of the pleasure and excitement out of the graduation ceremonies and made Betty feel resentful and sad.

The following September at Berkeley, the panic she had managed to keep buried at Smith became worse, and with it her asthma. She began questioning her commitment to psychology. In the 1940s most women did not aspire to any career. People generally believed that women were supposed to get married and raise a family. Those who did other things were either unnatural or could not get married.

In those years Betty believed that too. This belief was behind some of the decisions she made at Berkeley.

4

"A Real Job in the Real World"

At Berkeley the students were predominantly men. Betty thought they were no smarter than the girls she knew at Smith. However, there were many excellent scholars there who had come to study with Dr. Erik Ericson, a famous psychologist. (Dr. Ericson believed that human behavior could be understood only if all the different factors were taken into consideration.)

Betty's original plan was to do research and teach, perhaps become a great scholar like her professors. But she feared that choosing that road would lead to loneliness.

Loneliness was something Betty was much too familiar with. She knew she did not want to spend her life alone. And yet, what she was doing made her different than most women of her time.

Not only was it common for women to marry immediately after high school or college, but single women almost never lived alone or traveled alone. College was carefully chaperoned and supervised, with nighttime curfews and special passes for week-end leave. Boys who might come to visit were not allowed in the girls' rooms.

If a girl finished school and was not yet married she might take a job and live at home "until the right man came along." In face of all that established social custom, here was Betty traveling across the country to school. She was living independently in a university community dominated by men. The field she had chosen—human behavior—was one that few people understood.

Even though Betty was now a well-educated adult, it was not considered socially acceptable for her to visit or spend time with men unless there were older, married people to supervise and make sure there was no intimacy.

Betty was certainly aware of these social standards. She did not want to rebel against them or change them at this time in her life. What's more, she herself was afraid of intimacy with men, pushing it away when it was offered. Nevertheless, she did have some male friends from high school with whom she had kept in touch.

In the middle of her first year at the University of California, on her way home during Christmas vacation, Betty visited one of those old high school friends. He was now at medical school in Chicago. It was good to see him, to catch up on old news, and share future plans.

When she arrived home, her father was furious. Now he turned the full force of his familiar temper on Betty, accusing her of being immoral. How could she have done such an awful thing— visiting a man, alone. He was angry, disappointed, and ashamed of Betty.

Betty was appalled. Did her father understand her so little, trust her so little?

When it was time to return to Berkeley, Betty was still hurt and angry. She left without saying good-bye to her father, never suspecting that it would be the last time she would see him alive.

A few weeks later, Betty was called back for his funeral. Looking at the body of Harry Goldstein as he lay in the coffin, she could not forget their last encounter.

"I did not cry," she would recall years later, still trying to make sense out of her feelings.

When the funeral and the week of mourning were completed, Betty returned to Berkeley. She has written that she met a young man,

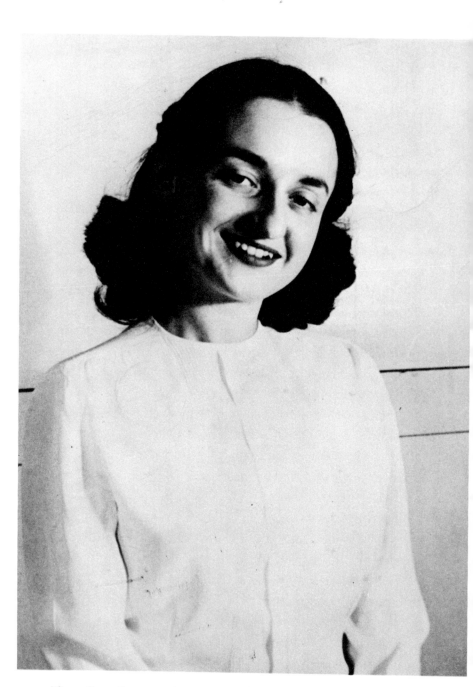

After college, Betty attended graduate school at the University of California in Berkeley where she studied psychology and met a young man.

and brushing aside any hesitations she may have had, the two became lovers.

The year was coming to an end, and Betty had been chosen for another fellowship. It would enable her to continue advanced research and get a Ph.D. in her field. But did she want it? In the 1940s most people assumed that you could not combine marriage with serious work. Was she ready to give up the love of a man, marriage, and children in order to pursue an intellectual career?

The answer came when Betty's boyfriend, a physicist at Berkeley, revealed his feelings. "Nothing can come of this, between us," he explained. "I'll never win a fellowship like yours."

For young women in the 1940s it was not surprising that a man would not take pride in his girlfriend's success. It seemed quite natural that men would want to feel smarter and more successful than their wives. Betty understood and agreed. These were her own doubts. Now they had been put into words.

Betty Goldstein refused the fellowship, never completely understanding why. She left Berkeley and gave up plans for a university career. She also left the man who had helped her make that choice. And now she had to decide on her next step.

Peoria was not a place to which she wanted to return. In spite of her scholarly successes which had been reported in Peoria's newspapers, Betty had not forgiven her hometown. Although none of her friends understood it, she had felt rejected there.

Those to whom she felt closest were her friends from college. Again Betty crossed the country, this time settling into a tiny apartment on Waverly Place, a street in the lower part of Manhattan Island, in an area called Greenwich Village. She shared the apartment with a group of college friends, including Harriet Vance from Peoria.

In the 1940s Greenwich Village was considered a neighborhood of nonconformists. That meant that many people who lived there disagreed with accepted ideas about how to live and what to think. Many were artists, writers, and students who were actively rebelling against the things most people believed. Some, like Betty herself and her friends, considered themselves to be radicals. They were concerned with the working class and with Negroes (as black people were referred to at that time).

New York was an exciting place to live in 1944 and 1945. There were new people to meet. There were theaters and concerts, lectures and rallies. And there was no lack of jobs. Since so many men had been drafted into the armed forces during World War II, women were needed to fill positions ordinarily filled by men. In addition, there were government agencies that had been formed especially to help the war effort and which were happy to hire women.

Betty, returning to her old interest in newspaper work, got a job for a small news agency. This agency, the Federated Press, reported on news that was of concern to labor newspapers. Although the job was not a challenge for Betty, and did not even begin to make use of her talents and intelligence, still she decided to take it. In those years it seemed to Betty that her achievements, instead of making her happy, were actually keeping her from finding love. She would try it this way.

But achievement had always been important for Betty. It was the way she had won approval from her parents and teachers from her earliest years. It was not that easy to give up.

Asthma plagued Betty. She developed a writing block and could barely manage to write the simplest stories. Betty realized that she needed help.

Psychoanalysis was becoming increasingly accepted. Perhaps once she understood her problems, the asthma attacks would stop and she would be a creative, productive person again.

But psychoanalysis required money—more money than Betty earned at her job at the Federated Press. In desperation, Betty appealed to her mother and told her that the therapy would help her asthma.

Harry Goldstein had left a substantial amount of money when he died. He had wanted Betty to manage his estate; he had even discussed it with her before that last terrible fight. Harry had feared that his wife would spend the money unwisely and there would be little left for his children.

Betty, however, had rebuffed him and refused. Money meant nothing to her then. Even if her mother would spend it unwisely, she wanted no part of it. Because her parents had fought so much about money, Betty preferred not to think about it at all.

Now, however, Betty had to look at money differently. It seemed more important and no longer something to be scorned. Money could be the key to her mental health and ultimately, her happiness.

Miriam, now remarried, agreed to give her daughter the money. Betty began therapy.

Although Betty's asthma did improve, and her writer's block finally disappeared, analysis was not the magic cure Betty had hoped to obtain. While it did help her to understand her relationships with her mother, and with men in general, she was still searching for love and dealing with the same problems.

Meanwhile, the world was changing quickly around her. In 1945 World War II ended. Young men were returning from the war and looking for work. Some wanted their old jobs back. Others found girlfriends, got married, and settled down to raise a family.

Betty lost her job at the agency; "bumped," as she put it, by a returning veteran. Shortly after, in January 1946, she was rehired for another position there and she accepted. It was not easy to find a job. She knew that she might be passed over in favor of any man who applied, no matter how capable and experienced she was.

The new position at the Federated Press did not work out well for Betty. She felt the supervisor was deliberately making it difficult for her. She was sure he wanted her to quit, and finally Betty did.

Betty took a similar job writing for a publication of the United Electrical, Radio, and Machine Workers of America, an electricians union.

In this office, Betty Goldstein learned many things about the problems of women workers. *UE* (as the union and the newsletter were

Shortly after Betty's marriage to Carl, the couple went on vacation in New England.

called) reported on a union campaign to achieve fair wages for women. *Equal Pay for Women: A Rate Based on the Job, Not on the Sex of the Worker* was the title of one of the pamphlets put out by the Federal government at this time and used by the union.

Whether conscious of it or not, Betty's ideas about women's place in society were developing here.

While Betty was changing her job, her friends' lives were changing too. Harriet was going home to Peoria to marry John Parkhurst. Maggie and Madelon, two other college friends, were moving on to husbands and the settled life they had all rejected just a few short years before.

Betty looked for another apartment. In spite of the serious postwar housing shortage in New York City, she did manage to find a place to live. It was small and dark and would have been unacceptable to some people, but Betty liked it. Tucked away in the basement of a town house on Manhattan's West 86th Street, she had to pass through the furnace room to reach her own apartment. It had no kitchen, and water pipes leading to the upper floors crisscrossed the ceiling. Still, it was her own.

Betty settled into her new job and her new home. It was just about this time that she met Carl.

Carl Friedan was one of the many young men who had returned from the army when the war ended. Although he had not graduated from college, he was intelligent and charming. During his college days he had worked part-time and summers as a magician and entertainer. In the army his job was to produce shows to entertain other soldiers. Carl had enjoyed that kind of work, and now he planned to organize a summer theater in New Jersey. One of his best friends was Betty's coworker, and so Betty and Carl met.

Betty liked Carl almost immediately. Her old interest in drama and acting made her feel that they had much in common. Betty liked the way he looked, and she felt comfortable with him. "He brought me an apple and told me jokes which made me laugh," Betty would later write.

Carl seemed ambitious and had lots of ideas that sounded exciting. He was ready to work but had not been able to find any place to live. Although it was not very common in 1947 for an unmarried couple to live together, Carl moved in with Betty. They shared the basement apartment with its brick wall, crisscrossing pipes, and tiny terrace.

Betty did not miss her privacy. At last she felt that she belonged to someone. This is what life was supposed to be about. Love and the right man would bring her all the happiness and fulfillment she needed. The psychological theorists insisted that this was true. All the stories in the women's magazines and on the movie screens promised "happily ever after" for young women who married and had children. Betty was sure she could succeed where her mother had failed.

In June 1947, Betty and Carl were married at City Hall.

5

"I Know This..."

"Marriage means togetherness," Betty had written in college. In one of her stories she had described marriage as a warm and happy situation, a closeness that would transform her and her husband into better people.

At first it really was like that for Betty. Despite some adjustments and differences, she liked being part of a couple. It was nice to share the evenings with a man. It was also good to have someone around to take care of things like repairs and to help with household decisions.

Three months after they were married, Carl and Betty took a trip through New England. They spent days sight-seeing, rowing on the lovely lakes, and hiking the mountains of Vermont and New Hampshire. They laughed and joked together and took snapshots of each other smiling happily.

Carl was originally from Boston. His parents still lived there, and part of this trip included a visit to her husband's family. Carl's mother had insisted on a traditional wedding, with a rabbi, done according to Jewish law. Betty and Carl agreed.

Betty was never sure what Carl's parents thought of her. On her first visit to her new in-laws, she had a terrible asthma attack. This physical condition continued to plague her whenever she had to face major problems.

The Friedans continued living in Betty's old apartment on West 86th Street. They had many friends and shared a busy social life. In addition, Betty was still politically involved with the same causes as before: fighting for justice for all people.

Although Betty continued to work, money was always a problem. Betty's paycheck contributed more than she would have liked to the family finances.

Carl tried running a summer theater and managing an off-Broadway theater group, but never made much money.

In spite of financial problems, when Betty realized she was pregnant she and her husband were pleased about the idea of being parents. Carl fixed up the tiny apartment so that it could accommodate a baby. Betty shopped for maternity clothes, took a leave of absence from her job, and planned for the future.

Although she and Carl had fights, it was easy to assume that this was part of being married. It was supposed to be up to the woman to make a happy home.

Then came Danny's birth, a joyous event that helped Betty forget her doubts. Perhaps it was true that a woman could only be fulfilled through marriage and children, Betty thought. Her interest in political matters became less important.

Danny was a constant wonder to her. Both she and Carl played with him, read to him, and helped him take his first steps. They watched him grow from babyhood and become a little boy.

During that time, Betty had gone back to work. In spite of her satisfaction with motherhood, adjusting to life at home was not easy for Betty. "It was obvious I wasn't as good at housekeeping as at my own work," she later wrote. She missed the intellectual challenge of work, recalling, "...I didn't have any more mental exercise than reading a detective story."

Betty had made a promise to herself, way back in high school. She

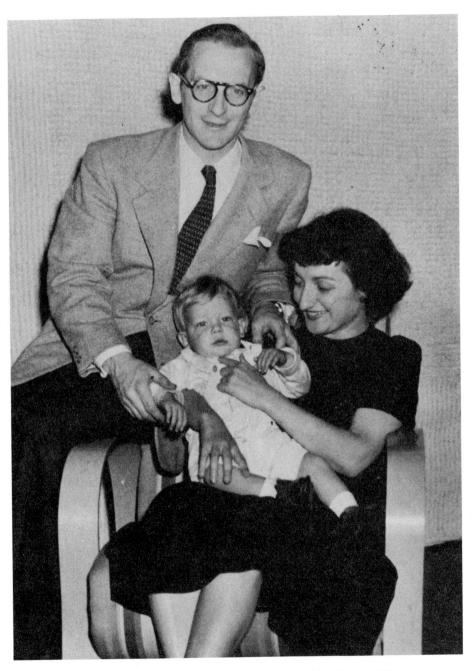

The birth of Danny was a wonderful experience for both Betty and Carl.

had written: "I know this. I don't want to marry a man, and keep house for him, and be the mother of his children, and nothing else..." She wanted a career, success, even fame.

A few years later, in an autobiographical essay written at Smith College, she reaffirmed that idea. She would "probably" marry... "but not someone who believes that women's place is primarily in the home."

Even without all those old dreams, Betty would still have needed to work. Carl seemed to have one business problem after another. After his involvement in theater, he found work in advertising. Although this new direction seemed more stable, they continued to be short of money. Most of Betty's salary went to pay the housekeeper, but there was some left to help with household expenses.

Then, when Danny was three years old, a second baby was expected. This meant more expenses and a bigger apartment.

Betty began the first of many searches to find the right place for the growing Friedan family to live. They were ready to leave the city. Betty reflected that once Danny was born, "we found we couldn't keep up with city friends."

Betty would prove to have a talent for discovering interesting and suitable homes. This time, in a newspaper advertisement, she read about a garden apartment development called Parkway Village, in Queens, a borough of New York City.

At Parkway Village the Friedans met other families and made friends. Their closest group was made up of six couples who also had children in the nursery school. The group baby-sat for one anothers' children and organized barbecue parties together. They planned a yearly seder. The six families even pooled their money to rent summer houses that they couldn't afford separately. These cooperative experiences would be repeated many times in Betty's life. They offered her the warmth of an extended family that she did not get from her own relatives.

Betty and Carl both wanted a large family. However, when their second son, Jonathan, was born they faced more debts.

Betty had lost her job as reporter for the *UE* newsletter when she was pregnant for the second time. The company did not want to give her another pregnancy leave. Even though the union contract allowed it, union members felt she was being unreasonable. With no support from the union, she decided not to fight.

Staying at home with her babies seemed more satisfying and necessary to her than a low-paying job, anyway. However, her financial problems and the tensions of her marriage continued. Her asthma attacks returned.

Betty's writing career did not stop when her job ended. She continued as a volunteer, composing articles for the Parkway Village community newsletter. Eventually she became its editor.

Although writing was difficult, sometimes even painful for Betty, she was very good at it and decided to try selling some articles. For her first effort, she chose a subject concerning suburban life — a subject she knew very well. After she researched and sold that first story, Betty acquired an agent, someone who would represent her and help her sell her work.

Now Betty began writing articles that were marketed to individual women's magazines. This method, called freelancing, was more successful than she had imagined. The best thing about it was that she could do it from home. She did not have to leave her children with a baby-sitter every day, and feel guilty.

Betty researched all her articles very carefully. As she became better known, she was given assignments by magazine editors, but she tended to write about the things she knew best.

One of Betty's early articles grew out of a conversation between her and her friend Gladys Carter. Was it good for mothers to work, or not? Betty claimed it was, whereas Gladys said staying at home was better. The two women wrote their opinions into an article and submitted it to Betty's agent, who sold it to *Charm* magazine.

Although her job as the mother of two little boys kept Betty from writing full time, she did manage four or five articles a year. The money she made helped with household expenses, and her success gave her a feeling of accomplishment.

Betty did not always enjoy routine household chores, but she adored her children and was proud of their achievements. As a mother she tried not to criticize them or suggest that she was disappointed with the kind of people they were. Having seen the unhappiness that attitude had created in her own family, she was determined not to repeat those same mistakes.

This resolution was easier to keep with her sons than it was with her husband. Yet in spite of their fights and difficulties, in 1956 Betty became pregnant again. With a third child on the way, she decided it was time for another move.

The 100-year-old stone barn in Sneden's Landing, about an hour from New York City, seemed just right. It was picturesque, romantic, and inexpensive. There was plenty of room for the children and lots of opportunity for Carl to use his home improvement skills.

Emily, Betty and Carl's first and only daughter, was born there. She was a lively and charming baby, prettier than Betty had been and more even tempered. With three children and a house in the suburbs, Betty and Carl seemed to be the perfect example of the American dream of the 1950s.

While the older boys were in school, Betty researched and wrote articles for magazines. After school, she car-pooled with all the other mothers, driving her boys to a variety of activites such as Cub Scout meetings, Little League baseball games, and friends' birthday parties.

Betty was happy with suburban life. However, the old barn at Sneden's Landing was difficult to maintain. It was cold and drafty and very expensive to heat. They kept the temperature down so that their heating bills would not be too high. Betty remembers typing her articles with gloves on during the winter they lived there.

So Betty looked around and was again successful. She found a large Victorian house in Grandview, New York. With the last $2,800 left from her father's inheritance, plus a generous loan offered to World War II veterans by the government, the Friedans managed to buy their first house. Betty would later say: "It was a wonderful house...on a knoll, and had a view of the Hudson River." She described it as an "old Charles Addams house," referring to the cartoonist Charles Addams who drew pictures of haunted houses.

The new house was large and rambling, with a big porch that circled the outside. Here, Danny and Jonathan would settle in to read or do homework on warm days. Inside there was a big fireplace for cozy winter evenings.

In order to save money, Betty went to auctions to find inexpensive furniture. For $25 she bought a used Victorian love-seat which became one of her favorite possessions.

In addition to writing, Betty again threw herself into neighborhood and school activities with all the other mothers. But as always, she wanted to — and did — make a difference.

As her children grew, and she became more involved in the school system, Betty had an idea. She remembered how eager to learn Danny had been when he was six. He could even "do long division in his head." But by the time he was nine, he was bored with school. Betty thought he could be a scientist, but realized he didn't know any scientists.

There were so many interesting and extraordinary people living here and in nearby communities, thought Betty. Why didn't the children have the advantage of learning from these experts as well as from their teachers?

With this idea in mind, Betty Friedan organized the Community Resources Pool, starting with a meeting in her own living room. This was the time when the Russians had just sent up the first *Sputnik* into space. There was a great deal of interest in improving science programs in schools, and other parents were enthusiastic.

Helped by friends, neighbors, and school officials, the project eventually received a grant of money from the New World Foundation and the New York State Education Department. After a few successful years, scientists, artists, writers, and politicians were asking to be part of it. They came into the schools to work with individual children or with groups.

The Community Resources pool was written up in all the newspapers. It was described as a "unique experiment in the enrichment of education."

Like her mother, Betty Friedan had boundless energies. While

Betty organized the Community Resources Pool to encourage interest in science in her children's school.

caring for her children, writing articles, and running the Resources Pool, she was also meeting a new challenge.

The year 1957 marked fifteen years since Betty Goldstein Friedan had graduated from Smith College. She was asked by the alumnae committee to survey her class, the class of 1942. The committee thought it would be interesting and useful to work up a questionaire. Its members wanted to examine how a Smith College education had affected women's lives.

Betty had resisted going to reunions before this. She always felt her achievements did not measure up to her early promise as a valedictorian of her high-school class. Her family had been told that she had the most outstanding record of any student who had ever attended Smith. What did she have to show for it?

Betty realized that she had "a question mark" in her own life. If she used her ability and education away from her home, she felt guilty. If she did not use her talents, she felt unfulfilled. What was the right choice?

Betty plunged into writing this questionaire. She spent much more time on it than the Smith committee had expected. Somehow she realized that in "hunting down" the responses of other women to this "question mark," she would find answers for herself.

6

The Search for the Feminine Mystique

"All I was trying to do with that questionaire," Betty later said, "was to show that an education wasn't *bad* for a woman, it didn't make her *maladjusted* in her role as wife and mother."

But in 1957 that idea was not so simple. Since the end of World War II, it seemed as though America was trying to convince women to stay at home and have babies and keep house.

Part of the reason for this was that many Americans had been killed during the war. People felt it was important to replace them with a new generation. In addition, the war had separated thousands of men and women. Husbands and wives had been apart, as well as younger people. They waited a long time to be together or to get married and raise families. Now that there was peace, they did not want to wait any longer.

Another reason why women like Betty were encouraged to stay at home had to do with the numbers of jobs available in America. Many women worked during the war. The country needed them to take the place of the men who had become soldiers. Women also worked in the factories that made guns, bombs, ships, and planes to help those soldiers fight and win the war.

Then the soldiers came back and needed jobs of their own. At the same time, with the war at an end, the arms factories were closing down. There were now even fewer jobs available and many more people to fill them.

These were just some of the reasons why it seemed right that women should stay at home. Other reasons had to do with what people honestly believed about the nature of the sexes.

"Women are naturally passive," wrote Lundberg and Farnham (Dr. Marynia Farnham was a psychiatrist herself). Women were meant to care for others, they believed. They needed husbands to protect them and to deal with serious problems such as finance, banking, and politics.

Just a little more than 100 years before, women had finally earned the right to own property. Less than 50 years earlier — just a few years before Betty was born — they had marched and protested and even gone to jail to gain the vote. Now, those courageous battles were all but forgotten.

In the rush to conform to the new ideas about being feminine, women who had an education and a chance for successful careers gave it all up. Betty herself had given up her career to marry and have children. The psychologists, the doctors, the women's magazines all promised that this was the way to find happiness.

The problem for Betty, and for so many other women like her, was that they were not satisfied. They felt there was something missing in their lives, but did not know what it was. As the doctors and specialists began to realize this, they searched for an explanation. Perhaps those dissatisfied women envied men. Could it be that they simply were not able to adjust to their own limitations?

Another of the many answers put forward to explain the unhappiness of some women was education. Women were getting too much education, or the wrong education, experts suggested. They were not being prepared for their role as wives and mothers.

Betty was aware of all this as she worked on the questionaire and interviewed her classmates. Forming the questions carefully, she tried to draw out as much information as she could. Fifteen years before, she had learned to do just that in her psychology classes.

"What difficulties have you found in working out your role as a woman?"

"What are the chief satisfactions and frustrations of your life today?"

"How have you changed inside?"

"What do you wish you had done differently?"

Betty's classmates laughed as they looked over her long and detailed list of questions. How like Betty, still the psychologist, to do something like this! Her classmates joked and reminisced, but they also took the time to give Betty the answers she was looking for.

Betty anticipated that her questions would reveal what she believed — that a woman's education *helped* her to be a good wife and mother. She arranged with *McCall's*, a leading woman's magazine, to write up the results as an article. When the reunion was over, she took the carefully filled out forms, said good-bye to many old friends, and returned home.

Back in Grandview, with the boys busy in school, and a part-time housekeeper to help with Emily, Betty looked over the results. What she found surprised her. More than that, she was astonished and excited.

Each one of the women who filled out her questionaire felt very much like Betty herself did. Each woman seemed to be asking the same question: "Is this all? Is this all there is to my life?"

Even then, a small seed of an idea was forming in Betty's mind. Could it be that the theories about what women needed were wrong? Was it possible for women to have more in their lives than motherhood and being a housewife?

Betty wrote and sent in her article suggesting these conclusions. It did not take long for *McCall's* to send it back. The editor, a man, simply did not believe it could be true.

50

Not discouraged, Betty sent it to another magazine and then another. No one, it seemed, wanted to publish her article. They believed that it was not what women wanted to hear.

Betty was not ready to give up. The results of this questionaire were too important, not only to her but to all women. Her thoughts turned to the possibility of writing it up as a book. During Betty's years as a freelance writer, she had gotten to know some editors. She knew they were always looking for interesting ideas for new books.

One of the most successful articles Betty had written was entitled "The Coming Ice Age: A True Scientific Detective Story." It was based on careful research about a recent scientific discovery. The story was printed in *Harper's* and then reprinted in *Reader's Digest*.

At that time, Betty's writing, as well as the interesting scientific ideas, had caught the attention of an editor at W.W. Norton & Co., a publishing house. He suggested that Betty might like to enlarge that article about the Ice Age into a book.

Betty thought it over carefully. It would be very nice to write a book. But not about the ice age. Geology was not a topic that Betty really cared that much about. Reluctantly, she turned down the offer.

Now, however, Betty had found a subject that she could call her own. Women's lives, her friends' lives, even her own life were at stake. She decided to return to W. W. Norton & Co. and ask if they were interested in her new idea.

It would take a year to complete, Betty had assured the publisher, and Norton agreed. When Betty left, she had a $1,000 check in advance and a promise of $3,000 more in installments while she was writing.

And now came the hard part. Using the scientific methods she had learned so well as a student, Betty compiled more questions. She set up interviews with women of all ages and studied the answers. She read about what different psychologists and researchers had said about the nature of women.

Betty also learned about the earliest heroines of the women's rights movement in America, such as Susan B. Anthony, Elizabeth

Cady Stanton, and Lucretia Mott. These pioneers had begun the first movement for equality back in the 1850s and '60s.

Going back even further, she read Mary Wollstonecraft's "Declaration of the Rights of Women." In eighteenth century England, Wollstonecraft had insisted that women should have the same rights as men. In 1958, few had ever heard her name.

The contemporary French writer Simone de Beauvoir had also written a book. Called *The Second Sex*, it analyzed women's second-class position in society. Ms. de Beauvoir's work was barely known in the United States either.

Betty found that up until World War II, women's magazines had praised the independent, career-minded woman. The women of the 1920s and '30s had seemed to benefit from the legacy of the women's rights movement. Now, in the 1950s, the great American women who had fought for women's suffrage (the right to vote) were more of a joke. There was even talk of reversing those hard-won rights.

All this information convinced Betty. There was something very wrong with the way society viewed women, and with the way women thought of themselves. They were not that different from men. Women were people. They wanted the same things as other *people*. Like Betty herself, women wanted husbands to love them and children to care for. But that wasn't enough for men *or* for women. They also needed and wanted challenges and goals and a sense of accomplishment outside the home.

Betty could understand that very well just by remembering her own life. "My own feminism," she wrote, "somehow began in my mother's discontent."

Even if a woman spent all her time raising her children, they would be grown up when she was in her forties, Betty realized. Then what? The problem of mothers being lonely and depressed after their children had left home was very common in American society. Betty could see clearly the reason for this.

"We had no image of our own future, of ourselves as women,"

Betty would write in her book. She began to understand that women were never encouraged to "grow up" the way men were. They never had to make career choices or plan for the future. They only planned up until the time they got married.

Most women wanted to be like other women and do what society expected of them. Planning careers or being in the work world was not considered to be truly feminine. Women wanted to be feminine, so they pushed away thoughts that did not fit in with that image.

"Women are encouraged...to answer the question 'Who am I?' by saying 'Tom's wife...Mary's Mother.'" Betty thought that was wrong. What's more, she believed it was this denial of her own personality that was making the American woman unhappy, empty, and somehow incomplete.

Betty first called the search to understand these ideas "the problem that has no name." Later, she herself named it: "The Feminine Mystique." She used the word *mystique* because "it means a whole body of myths and accepted truths that are not true."

The ideas and beliefs that had grown up about women were wrong, Betty was convinced. Trying to conform to them was making women unhappy. More than that, because of the mystique, society was wasting some of its best talent—the minds and hands of women.

It was not easy trying to explain all these ideas, proving them by using women's own words, and writing them down. The year Betty needed to complete the book stretched into two years. After three years she was still not ready.

Betty's papers and books were spread over the dining-room table in their Grandview home. A few days a week she traveled into New York City and used a desk in Carl's office, so she could work without interruption. She had often done this before, while working on her magazine articles. Later, she was given space in a special room for writers at the New York Public Library.

At those times, Betty would hire another woman to take care of her children. However, she always felt guilty about doing it. The

53

feminine mystique had managed to convince Betty, too, that her *real* place was at home.

As the fifth year of her work began, Betty knew she had to finish. She compiled and wrote and researched in every spare moment.

It had taken hours and years of hard work. Finally, in February 1963, the book was finished. *The Feminine Mystique* was printed and distributed in the bookstores.

Slowly, articles about her book appeared in papers all over the country. Betty was interviewed and photographed alone and with her family. She was invited to speak in many cities across the nation. Her ideas were discussed and analyzed and printed in large headlines.

"Time for Women To Be Humans," headlined one article. Another was named "Women Should Have a Mission." Still other reviewers claimed not to understand, or need, the feminine mystique at all. It just made women unhappy.

More important to Betty than the reviewers, however, were the ordinary women themselves, who were reading the book in large numbers. Letters from these women poured in, on the average of ten a day. Some told how grateful they were that Betty finally explained the roots of their problem. Others recounted the relief they felt, finally knowing that their feelings were shared by many other women.

Betty's favorite letters were those written by women who had read her book and gone on to change their lives.

Betty Friedan's own life was changing too. Lectures, columns for women's magazines, radio and TV interviews all made her feel proud of herself and important. In one interview Betty told the reporter: "A woman has to be able to say... 'Who am I and what do I want out of life.' She mustn't feel selfish and neurotic if she wants goals of her own outside of husband and children."

At home Betty's life was better than ever. Carl seemed genuinely pleased with her success. He even advised her publisher about how to publicize his wife's book.

When *The Feminine Mystique* was published, Betty's photo began to appear in newspapers and magazines throughout the country.

"It takes a strong man to enjoy his wife's accomplishments," Betty boasted in an interview later that year.

A few months after its publication, her book had made the best-seller lists. Carl and Danny, who was now fourteen years old, stopped into the local bookstore each day to check on how it was selling.

Betty was relieved and exhilarated by the events in her life. To celebrate, she purchased a dishwasher, had her living room painted bright purple, and bought new clothes.

7

It Changed Her Life

When Americans looked back to the year 1963 they would remember it as an exciting time. There was change in the air, and everywhere people were questioning old values.

In the South, black Americans were demanding equal rights. Both blacks and whites were coming down from the North into Mississippi and Alabama to help blacks fight for equality.

In many Southern cities, schools were being desegregated. That meant that for the first time, blacks and whites would share the same classrooms and school buildings.

Black people, insisting on their right to be served, "sat in" at local restaurants. "Whites Only" signs were no longer acceptable. There were also registration drives to ensure that black citizens were allowed to vote.

In Washington, D.C. a new young President, John F. Kennedy, was serving his first term. He seemed to care very much about equal rights and equal opportunity for all. President Kennedy organized the Peace Corps, which invited young Americans to go abroad and help people in undeveloped countries.

The President placed great emphasis on civil rights here in

America too. In 1961 he appointed a President's Commission on the Status of Women. Its purpose was to document the position of women in American society. The final report, issued in October 1963, found that there was discrimination against women in education and employment. Individual states followed the Federal government, forming state commissions on the status of women.

It was in this new climate of change that *The Feminine Mystique* appeared. "Why not civil rights for women?" people began asking. Women had a right to equal employment opportunities just as much as black citizens or any other citizens.

Betty Friedan had said it in her book. Women must be able to achieve "the full realization of human potential." No one would give it to them. No one had given rights to black Americans either. They had to fight for them. Betty's book began to make women — and some men — think about fighting for their rights as well. It made others very angry and frightened.

Betty had expected some negative reaction to her work. She knew the book talked about ideas that were different from the beliefs of most Americans. For this reason, critical reviews and comments did not upset her.

Personal attacks and rejection by people who knew her were more difficult. As the book became known, her own neighbors began to treat her with suspicion and hostility. Women with whom she had carpooled just a few months before now refused to drive her daughter to dancing class. They complained that Betty was too busy to take her turn driving, and would send a taxi instead. The other mothers were not happy about that.

Her children were left out when invitations were sent for friend's birthday parties. She and Carl, too, were no longer invited out socially. "I was a leper in my own community," Betty recalls.

What had happened? Betty believed that she understood. "I was too threatening to other mothers who hadn't yet come to terms with their lives," she later explained. "I was acting out the secret desire they did not yet dare to face in themselves."

In her book, Betty had written that women who did nothing but housework and child care were really unfulfilled. Children and husband are not the only things that define a woman, Betty insisted. She needs goals and challenges of her own.

This meant that women would have to start thinking very seriously about themselves. They would have to plan their lives differently, answering the difficult questions that, up until now, only men had to answer for themselves.

In the 1950s women did not need to question what they wanted to do with their lives. Career plans and choices about education and training were men's problems. Young women only needed to find husbands. A husband would then take care of his wife's needs, both financial and emotional — at least that is what people believed. Children and home were supposed to be the only fulfillment a woman needed. That was part of the feminine mystique.

When Betty, and other women after her, suggested that this was not true, it made some women angry and others frightened. One woman who read the book in 1963 remembered how difficult the experience had been for her. "All the assumptions I had always held about life were being challenged," she admitted. "I was in a panic."

The anger and suspicion that greeted Betty's book did not stop people from reading it. It encouraged more people to buy it.

Later that spring, Betty traveled to Peoria with her family. She went to attend her twenty-fifth high school reunion and to show Carl, Danny, Jonathan, and Emily her hometown.

Here on Farmington Road was where she grew up, Betty told her husband and children. And there, the Whittier Elementary School, the park in which she used to play, the library, the place where her father's jewelry store had stood.

The familiar streets and houses welcomed them. The people did not.

Betty thought that her friends and relatives were angry at her for what she had written. Her brother, Harry, greeted the Friedans alone. His father-in-law had taken the children out of town. He had been worried that "their radical aunt" would influence them.

That evening, at the banquet for the Central High School Class of '38, Betty remembered that no one would sit with her and her husband. Her friends remember the occasion differently. Harriet and John Parkhurst would later explain that there was simply no room at the table where Betty wanted to sit.

Betty and Carl had come to Peoria fresh from the success of her first book. She felt she was not treated like the celebrity she was. When she was introduced and called up to the microphone at the reunion, her words were angry and bitter. Some of her friends remember her saying: "All that I am today has nothing to do with Peoria." Her classmates were insulted, feeling that the good spirit of their reunion had been spoiled.

In spite of snubs by old friends and neighbors, both in Peoria and at home in Grandview, Betty was very much in demand. An explosion of invitations arrived in her mailbox daily. The new author crisscrossed the country, appearing at universities, before women's groups, and on television shows.

This meant that she would be able to spend less time with her family. Although she was troubled by this, she did not feel as guilty as she once had. In the past, she had made deals with herself about leaving her children. She would only do it if the article she wrote or researched made more money than it took to pay the baby-sitter. She didn't truly believe that she had the right to do it for herself.

One incident especially stuck in Betty's mind. When Danny was ten years old, she was a den mother for his Cub Scout troop. That year she gave up the honor of being included in a course for training television writers. She dropped out of the class because she felt guilty about missing her son's troop meetings. "Ten months later," Betty

Danny liked to do his school work on the big front porch of their home.

recalled, "Danny said apologetically that he hoped I wouldn't mind if he stopped going to Cub Scouts, it was too boring."

Betty had learned to put aside her guilt feelings. She believed her children could manage without her and hoped they would continue to be proud of her. She now had a full-time housekeeper and, of course, they had their father.

However, marriage with Carl was becoming more of a problem. At first, his excitement over her success improved their shaky relationship. But as time went on, Carl became more difficult to live with. In private the couple had terrible fights. Betty began to think seriously about ending the marriage.

Despite the fact that she could now support herself, the idea of divorce frightened Betty. No one she knew was divorced. There was no place in society for divorced women at that time. Other women looked at them suspiciously, worrying that they might steal their husbands. Betty knew that unmarried women were not included in social events. These were almost always limited to couples. Could she take the loneliness that a divorce would entail?

Betty put aside the question and concentrated on her work, and on changing her life in other ways.

After *The Feminine Mystique* the world would never be the same for Betty. Her book changed the lives of many women and of men as well.

Other events were also destined to affect the American people. The assassination of President Kennedy shocked the world. Civil rights battles were being won in the South, and new laws were being passed. The popular folk-rock singer Bob Dylan sang: "The Times They Are A-Changin'."

The spirit of change swept through households all over the country. Betty's book had made women think. Would it also lead them to act on their own behalf?

Betty herself was more active than she had ever been. Besides the many invitations to speak and lecture, she received an interesting proposal from the *Ladies' Home Journal*. This was one of the publications that had turned down Betty's original article about the feminine mystique.

Clay Felker, a consultant for the magazine, invited Betty to meet him at the prestigious Plaza Hotel's Oak Room. The Oak Room was an elegant restaurant, famous as a place for business lunches. Betty had often stopped in at the Oak Room bar with Carl in the evening.

At 12:30 Betty Friedan walked up the steps of the hotel, through the lobby of the Plaza, and into the dark-paneled Oak Room. Mr. Felker was not yet there, and Betty decided she would wait for him at the bar.

"No, madam, you cannot wait at the bar. Women are not allowed," said the waiter.

When Betty suggested that she wait at a table, the answer again was *no*. "We do not serve women in the Oak Room at noon."

She would not be permitted into the Oak Room at all! Instead, the waiter ushered her out and into another restaurant across the lobby.

Betty was confused and embarrassed. She wondered if perhaps she was not dressed properly. She had not known that women were barred from the Oak Room at lunch and could come in for dinner only if accompanied by a man.

Clay Felker had not been aware of this regulation either. He finally found Betty, apologized for the insult, and the two had their business lunch elsewhere. However, Betty herself felt insecure by what had happened. It took her a while to understand and then accept Clay Felker's offer.

Betty was being given the chance to be editor in chief of an entire issue of one of the leading women's magazines in the country. The *Ladies' Home Journal* offered her a free hand to examine women's experiences after *The Feminine Mystique*. She could invite anyone she wanted; women authors and poets, social scientists and psychologists who were in tune with the new image of women.

Betty hoped to offer to *Journal* readers some of the up-to-date and important ideas about women that the magazine's own editors avoided. Just a few short months before, an article in this very publication had insisted: "Man's biological function is to do, woman's to be." Betty had had enough of those outdated, false ideas about women. She planned to call the issue "Women: The Fourth Dimension," or "Beyond the Feminine Mystique."

Plans for the *Ladies' Home Journal* issue of June 1964 did not meet her expectations. In spite of the promise of its male editors to give Betty a free hand, they vetoed article after article. They also refused to use her idea of a "double-headed woman" on the cover.

Betty's new ideas contradicted the whole thrust and concept of women's magazines. Women's magazine editors believed that their audience was made up of women who wanted only to be housewives and mothers. They felt uncomfortable presenting ideas that might make them dissatisfied or angry enough to stop reading the magazine.

There *were* many angry letters from *Journal* readers in the months following Betty's issue. In response to the criticism, the *Ladies Home Journal* printed up another edition contradicting everything Betty's issue had stood for.

Clay Felker, who had first approached Betty with the idea, soon left the *Ladies' Home Journal.* He went on to become the successful editor of *New York* magazine. In a supplement to the December 1971 issue of *New York, Ms.* magazine was launched. *Ms.* was the first women's publication to be run by women, and was committed to full equality for all women.

The *Ladies' Home Journal* issue, edited by Betty Friedan, did attract many women who would never have read the magazine. However, it was a disappointment for Betty in many ways.

Her experience with the *Ladies' Home Journal* marked the beginnings of her public reputation as a woman with whom it was difficult to work. She herself admitted that staff members of the magazine labeled her "strident." Although Betty would make enormous contributions throughout her life, her brusque manner, impatience with others, and easy irritability would constantly drive people away.

Back home, Betty began to make some decisions about her family. It had simply become too difficult to live in the suburbs when both she and Carl spent most of their time in New York City. The children had no means of transportation and therefore no independence.

Danny and Jonathan, ages fifteen and eleven, were bright and active boys with many different interests, and Emily was already eight years old. Neither Betty nor Carl could make the time available to drive them where they needed to go.

Living in the city would mean not only that the children would be free to travel around by bus and train but that there would be more opportunities for them. The family decided it was time to sell their home.

Dale Bell, now a filmmaker in Hollywood, bought the old Friedan home overlooking the Hudson River. He remembers it as "a nineteenth-century fantasy, with three floors, turrets, and a porch."

When Mr. Bell first came to look at the house, it was Emily who showed him around. They passed through the bright purple living room and the study lined with bookshelves. He noticed labels on the shelves like "health," "education," or "divorce." These represented some of the many topics that were included in Betty's book. Betty had used this method to keep her work organized.

As Emily brought the prospective buyer up to the third floor she explained proudly: "And this is where my mother wrote *The Feminine Mystique*."

Installed in a roomy apartment in the legendary Dakota apartment house, in the heart of New York City, the Friedans found life very different. The children were registered in the highly respected Dalton School. Danny, although only sixteen, had already begun his college studies at Princeton University.

Many issues concerning women's rights came up during the

1960s. They crowded the agendas of political forums, from local and state legislatures up to the United States Congress in Washington, D.C.

In 1963 Congress had passed the Equal Pay Act. This was supposed to prevent employers from paying women less than men for the same job. In addition, the equal employment opportunity section of the Civil Rights Act of 1964 promised women the same opportunities as men. However, many women doubted that these laws would be enforced.

The Friedan's home in Rockland County, New York was where Betty wrote *The Feminine Mystique.*

Several years later Betty had a dream. In the dream she was "fooling around...evading some task, some appointment I was supposed to keep." She looked through a curtain and saw "thousands of women sitting out there on their chairs as if waiting for something, for some signal."

At first Betty thought the dream was telling her to finish writing her second book. Later she would understand that her subconscious was pushing her to organize American women to fight for their own rights as people.

8

"Reluctant Heroines"

The final commitment to organize a woman's movement came at the third National Conference of State Commissions on the Status of Women. It was held in Washington, D.C. on June 30, 1966. Betty Friedan was one of the women who went to Washington for that conference.

When Betty first arrived in Washington she met informally with many women who were employed by government agencies. Some worked for the EEOC (Equal Employment Opportunity Commission) itself. They were all dissatisfied with the way in which the laws for women were being enforced.

The Civil Rights Commission had hundreds of complaints that had been filed by women, Betty was told. Women were only being given token jobs in government. No woman had any real power. In addition, many women had been denied jobs or promotions after they had complained.

Although the government knew this, it was not doing anything about it. Most legislators did not consider fair employment practices for women to be a serious issue.

Even before the conference, a woman lawyer who worked for the

EEOC invited Betty to her office. She closed the door so that no one would overhear what she had to say. Then, close to tears, she urged Betty to "start a national organization to fight for women, like the civil rights movement for the blacks.... You're the only one who can."

Betty was still reluctant. Why doesn't the union organize? Betty asked. Or women government workers themselves? There were many answers to those questions.

The unions and the government were more interested in equal opportunities for black people now. Women's concerns were less important. Individual women who worked in the system feared they would lose their jobs if they protested too much.

Betty Friedan did not work for the government, or for anyone else. She was famous and respected. Still, she hesitated, preferring to try for action at the meeting of the state commissions.

During the conference, Betty met with a handful of women in her hotel room. They decided to present a resolution to the conference the next day. It would urge the EEOC to treat sex discrimination as seriously as race discrimination.

The following day, the commission gathered at a final luncheon at the Washington Hilton hotel ballroom. The women saw that they would be unable to get the resolution passed. They realized that they could do nothing at this conference; not change any policy, not pass any resolution. They had simply been invited to listen and talk and then return home. No results, no progress had ever been expected!

Betty was furious. Here was more evidence that women were not taken seriously. This time it was not just a minor injustice that brought out Betty's quick temper. This was something more important, something worthy of her anger.

The other women were enraged too. Right there at the Conference they began planning. Seated around a lunch table the group started to organize. While talk continued, Betty's mind raced ahead. She grabbed the only paper available at the table — the cocktail napkin in front of her — and proceeded to scribble.

"...to take the actions needed to bring women into the mainstream of American society, now. Full equality for women, in fully equal partnership with men. NOW — The National Organization for Women."

Those words became the statment of purpose of the new organization, which would indeed be called NOW.

Right there at the table, during the luncheon's official greetings and speeches, the women whispered to one another. Every few minutes, someone from Betty's table would scurry over to another table to ask a quick question or pass the word along. Government officials, who had refused to take action, sat directly in front of them on the dais. They knew nothing of the organization that was being born before their eyes.

From that day, Betty Friedan was launched on a new career. Besides being an author, she would be national president of NOW, an organization whose purpose was to fight for equal rights for women.

Among those joining with her were Dr. Kay Clarenbach, a professor from the University of Wisconsin, Mary Eastwood from the Justice Department, Dr. Nancy Knaak, a dean from the University of Wisconsin, Catherine Conray, a labor leader, and Carolyn Davis, director of the Women's Department of the United Auto Workers union. In addition, there were two people who were members of the EEOC: Aileen Hernandez and one lone male, Richard Graham. These people made up the first executive board of NOW. In all, there were thirty-two founding members.

The little group wasted no time. After a summer of recruiting, they moved immediately into high gear. The first step was a press conference announcing the formation of the new organization. Betty herself called it at her apartment in the Dakota. She explained to reporters that NOW "was a civil rights organization. Discrimination against women," Betty stressed, "...is as evil and wasteful as any other form of discrimination."

Immediately afterward, with an energy that far surpassed its limited numbers, NOW set up task forces, speakers bureaus, and committees. The women generously gave their time and money. They analyzed legislation that affected women, pointing out the places where it was unfair. They wanted to make people aware of all discrimination against women, not only in employment.

Groups and individuals lobbied in Washington, wrote letters, and made phone calls to Congressmen and heads of agencies. They kept reminding them that women lacked opportunities in sports and on television. Marriage and divorce laws were especially unfair to them.

As the group became known, more women flocked to join. They added their voices to the growing numbers who were pushing for change. By making women feel that they were not alone, NOW gave many of them confidence to do something about their own lives.

For some it was a time of revolution. Women who had dropped out of school to get married were now returning to finish their

Betty Friedan with other founders of NOW.

educations. Women of all ages were seeking employment outside their homes. Many felt very angry about all the lost opportunities and the injustices they experienced because of their sex.

Consciousness-raising groups were being formed too. In these small, informal groups women could join together to listen to one anothers' problems and learn from one another. Together, they hoped, they would have the strength to change their lives and their families' lives for the better.

Besides raising women's consciousness, one of NOW's first goals was to eliminate job advertisements that specified only women or only men. At the time it seemed like a very radical idea. However, Betty and the other executives understood its importance.

In 1966 it was widely accepted that women were good at certain types of work and men at other kinds. If an employer advertised for a secretary or a telephone operator, he automatically placed the ad under "Help Wanted, Female." If he wanted a maintenance person, an executive trainee, or an administrator, the ad appeared under "Help Wanted, Male." In this way, women were automatically excluded from many jobs that offered more opportunity and higher pay.

NOW members were convinced that this was unfair. They met with *The New York Times*, a major newspaper in New York City. The executive board refused to change its policy. Picketing the office did not have any effect either.

Feeling pressured to give too much too quickly, newspapers and other institutions began fighting back. They criticized NOW and its members, and made fun of them. Betty Friedan became the subject of political cartoons and the butt of jokes. "The Feminine Mistake," was one of the labels given to Betty and her book. She was jeered by columnists and commentators who found her appearance unattractive and her manners abrupt and brusque. In spite of all the negative criticism, neither Betty nor the other members were deterred.

Betty Friedan was used to disapproval. She knew she was a difficult woman and had been criticized even by her own supporters.

"I am nasty, I'm bitchy, I get mad," she admitted, "but by God I'm absorbed in what I'm doing."

In November 1967, NOW held its second annual convention. It was a historic occasion for the new organization, which would decide on its official "Bill of Rights" for women. Betty drew it up and wrote it out to be presented at the full session of the convention.

After much discussion, both open and private, NOW voted. The membership passed resolutions giving its official support to what would become major issues for women. One of these was maternity leave. This meant giving a woman the right to take a leave of absence from her job if she had a baby and to return to the same job. There were also commitments to tax deductions for child care, and money for educational aid and job training for women.

Betty insisted that passage of the Equal Rights Amendment be included in the NOW Bill of Rights. This amendment, first introduced to Congress in 1923, had still not been passed. The amendment was very simple. It read: "Equality of rights under the law shall not be denied by the United States or any state on account of sex."

Many women wondered how anyone could be opposed to such a bill. But there were bitter opponents to ERA and, indeed, to all new legislation for women. The opposition came from women as well as men. Many men feared equal rights would mean that their wives would prefer to be independent. They worried that women would leave their families and neglect their children. Some women were concerned about losing the special protections and privileges they presently had, such as the financial support of their husbands.

Although these issues had nothing to do with ERA, many people became confused about the meaning of this amendment. A few refused to support NOW's platform because of it. In spite of these fears, Betty insisted that passage of ERA must be part of NOW's Bill of Rights. Her opinion was accepted by the convention.

The item demanding that women have a right to choose abortion was more of a problem. Betty believed that abortion should be legal for every woman who felt she could not, or did not want, to bear a child. However, she was aware that this was a very controversial issue. She knew that if it was part of the NOW platform, many members would resign in protest.

As the first president of NOW, Betty Friedan preferred to have as large and as broad a membership as possible. She wanted NOW to include all kinds of women: political liberals and conservatives, young and old women, blacks, whites, and Hispanics. For this reason, she had considered not including the abortion issue in the Bill of Rights. However, there was so much strong feeling in favor of it that it could not be left out.

The right of a woman to choose abortion would later become one of the major issues for the feminist movement—indeed for all Americans. "A woman's right to control her own body" is still considered by NOW and most other feminist groups to be a civil rights issue.

After Betty had completed her term as president of NOW she would describe its founders as "reluctant heroines." "It is a mystery, the whole thing; why it happened, how it started," she wrote about those first years. "What gave any of us the courage to make that leap?"

During those busy years, however, Betty did not think about courage. She did what had to be done. It didn't really occur to her that she needed courage. Without fear, she faced the men who told her that she was wrecking family life and the women who accused her of denying motherhood.

Betty Friedan was a mother herself. She loved her children and knew she could be a good parent and still take part in work outside her home. With enormous energy and drive, she continued flying around the country, making speeches and organizing local chapters of NOW.

What concerned Betty was not only public pressures. She worried about the growing problems of her marriage and the bitter accusations from her husband.

Betty had once bragged that Carl supported her work. It takes a "big" man to be able to accept his wife's success, she told a reporter shortly after her book was published. But Carl did not enjoy being teased and called "Mr. Betty Friedan." He grew increasingly angry.

Betty too was angry. Carl's anger, coupled with Betty's, led to more fights. One of those fights occurred early in 1969. It was the night before an important event in the women's movement.

On February 12, NOW had planned to protest women's exclusion from the Oak Room restaurant during lunch hours. NOW decided that a large group of women would assemble at the Plaza Hotel that day just before noon and demand to be seated. Thinking ahead, they

Rome, Italy was one of the many cities to which Betty traveled to speak with women interested in forming their own women's movement.

informed the press and hoped to get as much news coverage as possible. Their goal was to make the public aware of the many unfair and exclusionary rules limiting women. Similar protests had been planned for other cities as well.

The women gathered outside the hotel early. They waited for Betty, who was to lead them in. The weather was cold and snowy and the minutes dragged by. Where was she? What had happened? Should they begin without her?

Finally, Dolores Alexander, a *Newsday* reporter and one of the women who knew Betty, made a few phone calls. She discovered the problem and urged the women to wait a little longer.

In a recent book on the history of the women's movement, author Marcia Cohen alleged that the Friedans' fight the evening before had resulted in several bruises for Betty. At first she considered not going to the protest. Besides being upset, how could she show up looking like this? But it was too important. Instead, Betty was persuaded to put on makeup and dark glasses to cover her black eye.

By the time Betty Friedan arrived at the Oak Room, a heavy snow was falling. She took her place at the front of the group and led the way inside. The women were dressed in their best; fancy dresses, gloves, even fur coats if they had them. They didn't want to give the management of the Oak Room any reason for refusing them admission to the oak-paneled restaurant with its glittery chandeliers and gleaming crystal.

In spite of their efforts to look their best and act in a dignified manner, the restaurant manager objected to their presence. They were refused entrance. When they marched in themselves and took seats at the empty tables, no one would serve them.

The group soon left, but not before the event was photographed for television and written up by reporters. The women had learned to use the media to their own advantage.

Although the women were turned away on February 12, their protest bore fruit. Shortly afterward, the Oak Room and many other restaurants abandoned their "men only" policy. Both New York and Pennsylvania passed laws forbidding discimination against women in public places.

Women were getting their business and law degrees. They wanted to be able to lunch where business was being done.

As for Betty, this was another victory for her and the women's organization she headed. However, her many public achievements could no longer divert her from the changes she had to face in her own life.

"It was much easier for me to go 'Rah! Rah!' with the movement," Betty later wrote, "than it was to change my own life personally."

That same year, she made the final decision for her divorce. Later she would realize that many of her decisions — especially her move back to New York — had been leading up to this inevitable conclusion. Still, it was one of the biggest challenges she faced. The idea of being alone and lonely in a world of couples scared her more than facing the most hostile audience or the harshest criticism.

Betty had been invited to speak in Zurich, Switzerland. She decided to go. "If I can manage being alone and eating dinners alone in another country," Betty thought to herself, "then I'll be able to face a divorce." In this way, her trip abroad became a test.

On her return, Betty Friedan went on another lecture tour to the South. During that time, she slipped off to Mexico and on May 14, 1969, obtained her divorce. From then on, she put the pain of her bad marriage behind her and, once again, actively set out to change her life.

9

"I Have Led You into History"

The divorce meant several kinds of changes for both Betty and her children. First, she had to sell the apartment in the Dakota. The money from that sale helped with the expenses of the divorce.

Then, Betty had to find a new home for herself and her family. This time, her choice was a rented apartment on 93rd Street, still in Manhattan, where her busy life was now centered.

But Betty wanted a quieter place, where she could relax with family and friends in a peaceful atmosphere. She found it in a beach house on the eastern end of Long Island, only two hours from the bustle of New York City.

The Hamptons was an area of Long Island where Betty and her family had often gone on vacation. She had shared summer houses before, first with her friends from Parkway Village and later with others. And she would not be alone here either.

Danny and Jonathan were both grown up by now. Danny was away at college and Jonathan was ready to be independent. Emily, only twelve years old, still lived with her. In addition, she would create a new family — what she later called "my extended family of choice" — with whom she could share her life.

After Daniel and Jonathan grew up, only Emily was left at home. With close friends, Betty created a new "family of choice."

That first "commune," as she referred to it, included several dear friends who were either divorced or alone for other reasons. They shared the house on weekends, holidays, and summers. They pitched in to do the household chores, made Thanksgiving dinner together, and brought out children and friends to be part of their group whenever they could. When one of them had a problem, he or she could turn to the others for comfort or advice. When someone was angry, he or she would fight or criticize and then forget about it, just as family members do.

Betty's commune saw her through many difficult times and cheered her on in her successes. Over the years, the commune family changed. New people joined and then drifted away. However, that first group is still counted among Betty's closest friends. With their support Betty made some of her most difficult decisions, both in her personal life and as president of NOW.

The women's movement had been expanding throughout the four years of Betty Friedan's presidency. Her ideas were catching on and spreading to include women from different walks of life and from all parts of the country.

Airline stewardesses were clamoring for job security and demanding that the airlines change their rules. Women who aspired to be astronauts were suing NASA (National Aeronautics and Space Administration) for the right to compete to go into space. Female high school students were suing their schools, insisting that they had a right to take shop classes as did male students.

NOW supported these causes and many similar demands. Betty and the rest of the board never lost sight of their commitment to full equality for women in every aspect of life. But while there was a great deal of progress and change throughout the United States, feminists were still concerned.

Richard Nixon, the man who had become President of the United States in 1968, seemed less sympathetic to women's issues and causes. His disinterest, NOW leaders understood, might lead to a decrease of interest by the government. There would be less commitment to work for women's rights and a loss of momentum.

In 1970 President Nixon showed his lack of concern for improving the status of women by nominating G. Harrold Carswell for Supreme Court Justice. Many people believed that Carswell had a judicial record of sex and race discrimination.

When Betty heard that Judge Carswell had been chosen by the President, she was outraged. In one of his decisions, this judge had ruled that an employer had the right to refuse to hire a woman who had children under six years old. With a man like that sitting on the highest court in the United States, Betty realized, women had little chance of getting their legislation through the courts.

In a letter addressed to President Nixon, Betty explained some of the reasons why she objected to Carswell's nomination.

"Over 25 percent of mothers with children under six are in the labor force," she wrote.

"Eighty five percent of them work for economic reasons. Over half a million are widowed, divorced, or separated. Their incomes are vitally necessary for the support of those children."

Betty decided that she would be one of the people who would testify against Judge Carswell. At the Senate hearing, she repeated the facts she had written to the President. To these she added many other reasons why she felt Carswell would be an unsuitable Justice.

During her testimony Betty suggested that perhaps a woman should be nominated for the Supreme Court. Some of the Senators at the hearings laughed outright at this suggestion, considering it to be just another wild, feminist idea. They could not guess that only twelve years later, there would be a woman Supreme Court Justice, Sandra Day O'Connor.

After Betty testified, she called another of her many press conferences. In her living room she assembled a varied group of women. They included members of the YWCA, the Democratic and Republican parties, a woman from a radical consciousness-raising group, and a leader of a group of black welfare mothers. She would show the country that all women were united on this issue! Together, women had the power to fight against appointments that ignored their concerns.

A few of Betty's friends in Washington later told her that "the fuss made by women" had really made a difference. Because of the "unexpected pressure" from women all over the country, Judge Carswell was not nominated to the Supreme Court.

Betty began to see even more clearly that despite their differences, women could unite and work together on issues of shared concern.

In spite of Betty's insistence that she could accept opinions that conflicted with her own, it was not always easy. Often, other women's suggestions about how to fight for equality were completely opposed to her goal of "equality for women in equal partnership with men."

Betty's belief that "men are not the enemy" and that women must work together with men had been accepted without question by the NOW founders. But by the late 1960s there was a whole new group of women with different opinions, who were speaking out. These women sometimes felt that men *were* the enemy. A few even spoke out against marriage and families, insisting that women did not need men for anything.

Although Betty might once have considered herself a radical, she neither understood nor sympathized with these ideas. "Murky new currents" was the phrase she used to describe both the women and their programs for change. In spite of her discomfort, however, Betty could not prevent the newer groups from influencing the women's movement. Her differences with them would lead to many problems.

By 1970 it had become clear to Betty that she could no longer be the president of NOW. Organizing and speaking for NOW had taken up almost all of her time. It had also used up a great deal of her money, since she had to pay her own travel expenses. Betty felt she needed to get back to writing and earn some money to help pay the rent. Now that she was divorced, there were no longer two incomes to pay household expenses.

Another reason why Betty decided to step down was that NOW vice president, Aileen Hernandez, wanted to run for president. She was a good administrator, and Betty had faith in her ability as a leader. She was also a black woman, and as president she would help to quiet the criticism that NOW was an organization of only white middle-class women.

With the decision to end her official leadership, Betty's responsibility for the movement and its goals did not end. On her way to Chicago, Betty made a sudden decision. What was needed, she thought, was an action to show the country how powerful women really were.

"All those women across the country were ready to identify with the women's movement," Betty felt sure. They just needed something to do that was simple and forceful. They needed a march — a women's strike.

When her plane landed at the airport in Chicago, Betty told a few of her colleagues in NOW about her idea. Then, without waiting for approval from the board, she began making plans, setting a date, and thinking about a committee. She included the idea in her speech and presented it to the members of NOW at the convention.

Betty's final speech as president of NOW was long and memorable. Her friend Kay Clarenbach teased her, telling her she spoke "like some Communist commissar" for over two hours. Betty herself was exhausted when she finished talking. Her final words were: "I have led you into history. I leave you now — to make new history."

Betty got a standing ovation from the audience for her speech. However, some of the board members were angry. She should have consulted them before she announced a march for August of that same year. They felt it would be a waste of NOW's resources. If it failed, the organization would be embarrassed, they insisted. The new president, Aileen Hernandez, did not want to take the risk.

She would take the responsibility — and the blame if it failed — Betty insisted. And besides support from NOW, she would seek help and support from all the other women's organizations that were spreading across the country. She had said in her speech the day before, "our sisterhood is powerful." She meant to prove it.

Back home, and on weekends in Long Island, Betty set the wheels in motion. With the support of her family of friends and her daughter, Emily, she made phone calls, contacted other organizations, and recruited marchers. She even raised money with a fund-raising party in the Hamptons that attracted a lively mix of social celebrities, writers, and artists.

Betty and her small group of workers printed up leaflets and flyers, distributing them throughout the city in the busiest neighborhoods. Articles found their way into newspapers. Betty asked, and got, the mayor's support.

The march was also sponsored by some of the most important women leaders in the city. In addition, a whole range of women's organizations was helping with the work, from the Radical Feminists to the YWCA to the National Coalition of American Nuns. Arrangements with the city's police and traffic control were going ahead. Buses were chartered to bring women in from suburban areas.

Finally, the day of the march arrived. Betty had chosen this date, August 26, 1970, because it was the fiftieth anniversary of the Nineteenth Amendment, the women's suffrage law. In 1920, after a twenty-three-year struggle, women had finally won the right to vote.

They had taken to the streets then too. Women had spoken out and protested, defying fathers, husbands, and even the police. Some had gone to jail because they believed in women's equality. When the battle was finally won, the protests ended and women went back to their homes and their jobs.

Today they were being asked to march once again. Would the

84

women respond to this call? Many doubted it. Some expected only a small turnout.

Betty worried. She had set up a budget of $10,000 for NOW, much of it to be raised at a victory celebration afterward. If the march failed to attract enough women, this fund raiser would also fail. Still she was hopeful.

"I have a sense that there are a lot of women out there," Betty insisted. She believed that many more women would join in.

Rallies and speeches were planned throughout the morning and afternoon. They were well attended and successful.

As the day progressed, the crowds of women grew larger and the traffic jams worse. Betty took a bus uptown to Central Park. That was where the women were assembling for the big march. Glancing at her watch, she realized it was dangerously close to 5:30 P.M., the time they were scheduled to begin.

With cars at a standstill, Betty made a quick decision. She jumped off the bus and headed toward the park. She could walk faster than the bus could move through this traffic.

As Betty approached the meeting place, she hardly believed her eyes. As she later described it: "There was a sea of people waiting to march." They filled the park and the sidewalks and spilled over into the streets. The women had answered her call.

Mayor John Lindsay was there too. Like many others in the city, Mayor Lindsay did not believe there would be such a large turnout. He had told the women they would have to stay on the sidewalk. Well, there was no way that all these women could stay on the sidewalk.

As the march began, with Betty at its head, she shouted as loud as she could: "Take the streets!"

Ignoring the New York City rush-hour traffic, and the policemen, she moved toward the middle of Fifth Avenue. Thousands followed her, pouring out of Central Park and filling the broad avenue with a solid wall of marching women.

Betty planned the woman's march because she wanted to offer women something simple and forceful to show their support of the women's movement.

"Come join us, sisters!" the women called to those watching from the sidewalk.

"March with us."

And they did join, squeezing in among the more than 10,000 marchers, carried along with the throngs. Women forgot that they had been rushing home to prepare dinner, pick up a child at the baby sitter, or meet a friend. This seemed to be more important just now.

Secretaries and housewives; lawyers and typists; museum workers and waitresses; women of all ages linked arms in a symbolic gesture of unity. Grandmothers, mothers, and daughters walked together carrying banners proclaiming: "Equal Rights — to Jobs and Education," "Twenty-Four-Hour Child Care," and "Political Power to the Women."

There were men too, marching to support their mothers, wives, and children. A few carried signs that said "Men for Women's Rights."

It was a long walk and the August weather was hot, but to Betty it seemed like minutes. Soon she saw the majestic lions that flanked the granite steps of the giant library on 42nd Street and Fifth Avenue where the march would end. She led the women around the block to the green area of Bryant Park, behind the library, one of the busiest corners in the city.

Now it was time for Betty Friedan to speak. Wearing a raspberry colored shift, her shoulder length hair graying, she climbed slowly up to the podium and looked down at a sea of faces. How beautiful these women were! Every woman looked strong, capable, and courageous, Betty thought. They all seemed to be six feet tall.

As the crowd cheered, Betty began her speech.

"After tonight, the politics of this nation will never be the same. By our numbers here tonight...we learned...the power of our solidarity, the power of our sisterhood."

From somewhere deep within, came a phrase from her own tradition. She altered the ancient Jewish prayer to end with these proud words: "Thank thee, Lord, that I was born a woman, for this day."

10

"What Is the Women's Movement All About?"

The Women's Strike for Equality, its sheer excitement, its success, remained forever as one of the high points in Betty's life. Years later, Betty would reminisce about the wonderful feelings she experienced that day. However, she also marked it as the end of the movement's "three golden years."

At that march, Betty wrote, "we discovered...that 'sisterhood is powerful.' But after August 26...the women's movement became the target—the vulnerable, even willing victim—of others' political and economic ripoffs..."

Betty meant that women allowed themselves to be diverted from the real issues. Instead of fighting together for child care, equal pay, and equal opportunities, some women were manipulated into supporting other causes.

A few women used the women's movement for their own careers. This caused deep divisions among the different women's rights groups and prevented them from successfully working together.

Betty felt that the second march in New York City was an example of those kinds of divisions. Others denied it, claiming that Betty was unable to work with other people and didn't understand the issues.

The second march had been scheduled in those first heady days after the August strike for equality. The idea behind it was to continue pressure to enforce the new civil rights laws protecting women. Betty had set up a committee — a coalition of all the different women's groups — to plan the second march. She herself was traveling and speaking and not involved in the details. The march was scheduled for the end of the year, December 12, 1970.

One of the things the committee voted to do was show their support for lesbian women (women whose sexual preference was to love other women). The women on the Coalition committee believed that whatever a woman's sexual preference, she still had the same rights as anyone else.

The decision was made. During the December strike for equality, all the women in the march would wear armbands of lavender, the color that symbolized lesbians. Along with the armbands would be leaflets explaining that "we stand together as *women* regardless of sexual preference."

When Betty was handed an armband and a leaflet at the march, she was shocked and angry. She took her place on the platform and made her speech. But when the program was over, Betty could not contain her fury. Her colleagues had used her name to help a cause for which she had no sympathy. Worse still, they had done it behind her back.

Betty was sure that mixing women's issues with the controversial question of sexual preference was a terrible idea. It was the worst thing that could happen to the women's movement — her movement.

"This is not a bedroom war," Betty had insisted. When other feminists condemned men, or supported the idea of women loving women, Betty repeated over and over: "Men are not the enemy."

The Women's Strike Coalition quickly disappeared and most people forgot what had happened. For Betty the incident was a bitter disappointment and a turning point; the point when the women's movement took on a life of its own.

This event marked the beginning of a series of unsuccessful efforts for Betty. It also caused a rift between her and Gloria Steinem, a well-known journalist and one of the new leaders of the Women's Strike Coalition. One year later, Gloria would become a founding editor of *Ms.* Magazine.

Many people preferred to work with Gloria than with Betty. Gloria's gentle manners and striking good looks made her a desirable model for women and for the women's movement. She was also more sympathetic to the radical demands of the younger feminists.

Betty Friedan and Gloria Steinem soon clashed again in the interests of feminism. It began with an idea that seemed to come simultaneously from many different sources. The idea was that women needed to organize within the political structure and help elect more women to Congress. These women would then have the power to further women's rights.

Not only Betty, but Bella Abzug, the feminist Congresswoman; Shirley Chisholm, the black feminist who later ran for President; Gloria Steinem; and others all saw the need for this kind of organization. It would help women get into the political mainstream.

Betty, with her usual energy, plunged into the work of organizing. Before long she had contacted women throughout the country from both political parties to form a new group called the *National Women's Political Caucus*.

Bella Abzug, another founder of the caucus, had other ideas about how to organize. She was as forceful as Betty and was not ready to allow another person to make decisions without her. Bella told Betty that she should have been notified first. *She* was the one in Congress, and she knew best.

Bella's close ally in this project was Gloria Steinem. Steinem and Abzug insisted that other women be given a chance to be heard and seen in the new organization. They wanted to strengthen a coalition of the poor, the young, minority groups, and more radical elements by making them the center of the political caucus. Openly, they told Betty that her face was seen too much in the media. It was time to make room for others.

Betty also believed, as she later wrote, that the women in the political caucus should represent "all political elements, from young and black and radical to white-haired Midwestern Republicans." She felt that her rivals wanted to eliminate the Midwestern Republicans and keep only the radical elements. This policy, Betty was convinced, would just create another women's group that could be used by the political left. It would not be — as she wanted — a broad-based movement that would work to help women.

Until the end, Betty insisted that Bella Abzug and Gloria Steinem wanted to use the National Women's Political Caucus to gain more power for themselves. She first accused them of manipulating the organization at the Democratic Convention in Miami in 1972. The argument concerned the question of whether or not the women of the caucus would meet as a group to decide who to support.

In a showdown with Gloria at that convention, Betty admitted shouting at Steinem while the younger woman "said sweetly... that I had to get out or else." This open conflict clearly showed the different styles of the two women. It also confirmed their opposing positions within the women's movement.

Betty continued working to help organize the caucus in New York State and nationally. But she remained distrustful of Gloria Steinem and Bella Abzug, and she was angry when the caucus refused to support some important women candidates.

Finally, at the national organizing conference in Houston, Betty claimed that the election results were altered so that she would not be part of the caucus steering committee. Betty was so convinced that the voting had been improper that she hired a lawyer. The lawyer presented Betty's accusations and evidence to the next caucus meeting. However, in the end, she was not ready to take her case into court and challenge the women's movement. She allowed the issue to be dropped.

Many agreed with Betty, believing that the political caucus was being taken over by radical groups. Other women shrugged off Betty's criticisms. She couldn't get along with anyone, they said, and always wanted to run the show.

Betty herself admits to having been outmaneuvered in the political caucus by Gloria Steinem. As she later wrote, "I was no match for her." Gloria's good looks "somehow paralyzed me," she confessed. The contrast in the two women's appearances did not escape the press

WOMEN MUST HAVE A REAL VOICE AT THE DEMOCRATIC CONVENTION
Vote June 20 For

BETTY FRIEDAN
for Democratic Delegate
19th congressional district

You have 7 delegate votes— use one for Betty Friedan

Betty gave up her idea of going into politics after her struggle with the National Women's Political Caucus.

either. It made the most of the rift between them, claiming that Betty was jealous of Gloria because she was blond and pretty.

Betty did not see it that way. She would write of her feelings about Steinem. "...My battles with Gloria...involved my most basic sense of what the women's movement was all about."

One of the results of Betty's losing battle over the National Women's Political Caucus was her own withdrawal from politics. Before the 1972 elections, she had been a candidate for delegate to the Democratic convention. For a while she seriously considered running for the Senate from New York State. But after seeing what happened during the elections at the caucus steering committee, she realized she was too "timid" for politics.

The National Women's Political Caucus did succeed in its first few years. From 1973 through the end of the decade, many women were elected to local, state, and national office. Betty Friedan was not among them.

In spite of Betty's convictions about equal rights for women, her past successes, and her fame as "Mother Superior to Women's Lib," these disappointments bothered her and perhaps contributed to a low period in her life.

Another factor affecting Betty's self-image at this time was her age. On February 4, 1971, Betty Naomi Goldstein Friedan celebrated her fiftieth birthday. She was traveling in England at the time. February 4 had been such a busy and exciting day, that she had forgotten all about its special significance. When she realized, it was almost a relief. "What's the point of making it if you can't celebrate being fifty?" That was the question she asked herself later, in her second book.

However, between the moment of realization and the reality of growing older, there were a great many feelings to work out. Betty began to question herself, and her journals show a period of soul searching—even depression—at this time. Except for a handful of close friends, the women's movement seemed to have forgotten Betty. Betty herself admitted that she felt very far away from some of the problems presently addressed by the women's liberation movement. "Women's lib" was the popular term for the women's movement. Betty always preferred "women's rights." "Women's lib" was generally associated with students and more radical, younger women.

Betty thought that the organized women's movement was being overly influenced by these groups. She felt that they were trying to change the reality of women's lives too much and were ignoring the importance of the family.

In 1971 a new feminist publication was formed with Gloria Steinem as a founding editor. It was called *Ms.*, the title being used for women instead of *Miss* or *Mrs.* The idea behind using *Ms.* was to avoid identifying women by their marital status.

Betty Friedan was not on the editorial staff of *Ms.* She had never even been asked to write an article for them, although she wrote for many other publications.

Betty later commented: "It didn't interest me to talk to the already-convinced." She chose to write a monthly column for *McCall's*, an older and more conservative woman's magazine. She called her column "Betty Friedan's Notebook." Each month Betty reported on her thoughts about the development of feminist ideas throughout the country. She also wrote about her own life, explaining: "Everything I know has come from my own experience."

When, in 1973, Betty traveled to Rome for an audience with Pope Paul in the Vatican, she told her *McCall's* readers about it. Her article described how she prepared for the visit, what she wore, and what she and the Pope talked about. She urged Pope Paul to "come to terms with the personhood of women."

Betty's writing was almost always positive. She saw the gains and the successes for women first, before admitting the problems and needs. This optimism often made other feminists think that Betty Friedan cared only for the fortunate few who had already "made it." She was accused of ignoring the problems of minority and poor women. New feminist leaders blamed her lack of understanding on her middle-class values and criticized her for having a black woman housekeeper.

In spite of Betty's optimistic outlook on women's progress, she continued to be very pessimistic about herself. Invitations to lecture all over the world and to teach at one university after another did not make her feel better.

Shortly after Betty's divorce from Carl, she had gone to Esalen in California and was pleased with the results. Esalen was a method of

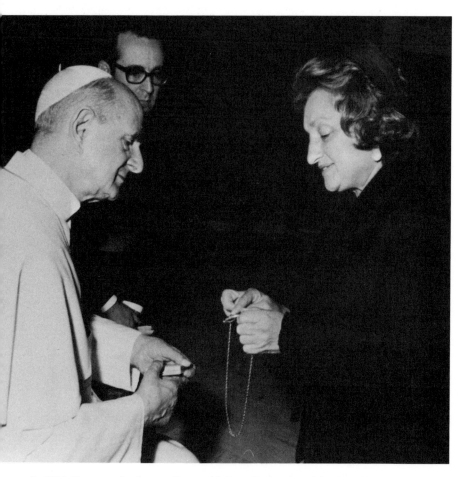

In 1973, Betty received an audience with Pope Paul and explained to him the goals of the women's movement.

group encounter that was very popular at the time. It promised people more self-awareness and an improved ability to relate to others.

Now, she again felt that her personal difficulties were serious enough to affect her work. As in the past, her problems caused a writer's block. Her second book, long overdue, was not yet completed. There had been a few men in her life, but none had developed into the permanent relationship that she wanted.

Self-doubt plagued Betty, and loneliness too. Her two sons were off on their own. Of course there was her daughter, Emily, and the close friends in what she called her extended family. They helped Betty through the toughest times. But it was not enough.

Betty began going to a new kind of group encounter. This group promised self-awareness as well as self-purification. Members of the center tried to help one another to deal with and change their lives.

Slowly, Betty began to understand herself better and to work her way out of her depression. She gained the strength to face the anger she had toward her parents and, finally, to end another unhappy love affair. At the same time, Betty also began to examine her roots and rethink her relationship to her Jewish tradition.

The new search into Judaism was partly because of her son Jonathan, to whom she had always felt very close. Jonathan had visited Israel and had begun a study of Jewish Law. Betty also wanted to learn more about her religion and culture.

She visited Israel in 1972 and undertook her inquiry into Judaism with the same energy and enthusiasm she devoted to everything. "The passion against injustice, which made me address myself to the problems of women," Betty realized, "probably had its roots in my own earliest experiences as a Jew..."

Despite the fact that on her first visit to Israel Golda Meir (then prime minister) refused to see her, Betty returned several times. She participated in joint conferences with Israeli women and encouraged the formation of a small group of Jewish feminists there.

It had not been easy for Betty to be Jewish. In Peoria, she claimed,

Jewish people often "changed their names and did something with their noses." Betty had done neither of these things. Now she was discovering the positive and meaningful values of her tradition. She saw herself as a "social prophet."

As Betty later wrote: "Having confronted our authentic identity as women, we who were Jewish began to confront our authentic identity as Jews."

As an early and outspoken leader of the women's movement, Betty Friedan was internationally known. She was invited to Iran in 1974 to speak to the Woman's Organization of Iran, which was founded by the Shah's (King's) twin sister. Betty's fame in America enabled her to have an audience with the Shah of Iran and his wife during her visit.

The same year she went to Iran, Betty became a Chubb Fellow at Yale University. This appointment was a prestigious honor.

An invitation to Iran in 1974 was part of the Shah's attempt to liberate Iranian women. Betty met with the Shah's wife.

Less than two years later, Betty's second book came out. *It Changed My Life* did not have the impact that *The Feminine Mystique* did, but Betty kept going. She began planning for a third book, this one about aging.

Finally, in 1975, Betty was invited to her alma mater, Smith College, to receive an honorary degree. She considered it a long-over-due honor. Gloria Steinem, who had graduated from Smith fourteen years after Betty, had already been honored in this way three years before.

The two women's names would often be included in the same lists as leaders of the women's movement. Betty Friedan had been named (together with Gloria Steinem) as a Woman of the Year by the *Ladies' Home Journal* in 1972. Both appeared again in 1978 among the twenty-five most influential women in America.

Betty continued lecturing and writing too. But an article she wrote in *The New York Times* in 1978 was greeted with fury by many feminists. They claimed the philosopher of the woman's movement had "sold out."

In this article, called "Cooking with Betty Friedan....Yes, Betty Friedan," Betty wrote: "No, I am not announcing public defection from the women's movement." But, she asked, "Why did I lose touch with those particular female roots of my own, those generations of women who expressed their love with chicken soup? Was it really all bad?"

Through a barrage of criticism, Betty continued her work, convinced that she was right. What's more, as she claimed in her book *It Changed My Life*, she was no longer "miserable and shrinking inside."

She was well aware that by the mid-1970s, hundreds of thousands of women had raised their consciousness and had returned to work and to school. Now women were getting ready to push for passage of the Equal Rights Amendment.

The press might criticize her, other feminists might ignore her. But Betty Friedan knew that she had started it all.

11

The Struggle for ERA

The decade of the 1970s was an important time in the history of the women's movement. There had not been so much legislation or so much talk about women since they had gained the vote back in 1920. Now, fifty years later, women's rights had again become the issue of the day.

Beginning with the Women's Strike for Equality in 1970, new laws concerning women multiplied. That same year the United States Department of Labor issued guidelines against sex discrimination. With the guidelines in place, NOW filed sex discrimination suits against 1,300 corporations and 300 colleges.

The following year, 1971, the Supreme Court ruled that businesses cannot refuse to hire women with small children. Then in 1972 the Equal Rights Amendment (ERA) was passed by both houses of Congress, allowing seven years for the individual states to ratify it.

Feminists were excited and optimistic. Many believed it was just a matter of time before all the reforms in the feminist platform would become law. There was talk of a woman in the White House; a woman on the Supreme Court. A woman's name—Frances "Sissy" Farenthold—had been placed in nomination for Vice President at the

Democratic Convention of 1972. Although she had not been nominated, she had received a large number of delegate votes.

In 1973 there was more cause for optimism. The famous *Roe vs. Wade* decision ruled that abortion would no longer be illegal in the United States. In addition, twenty two states had already ratified ERA by the beginning of 1973. All that was needed was a total of thirty-eight, and there were several years left to accomplish that goal.

International interest, too, had been awakened. The United Nations was becoming aware of women's rights as an important world issue. It declared a Decade of Women, beginning in 1975, and lasting for ten years. During that time, individual countries would study the roles and problems of women in their own societies.

The decade would be marked by three international conferences on women. The first, scheduled to open up the International Year of the Woman, was held in Mexico City.

Even before the conference got under way, Betty began to be aware of problems among the different factions and political groups. She had gotten several letters warning her not to speak where she was "not wanted." The letters threatened that she would be denounced as an American and a Jew if she went to Mexico.

Betty never discovered who had written those letters. But there was never any question in her mind that she would attend the conference. She went ahead with travel plans and conferred with the women from NOW and with other women's organizations.

Betty had not been chosen by the government as a delegate. She was attending as a member of the press. However, she had been invited to speak at the Tribune of nongovernmental organizations, which was meeting nearby.

In her speech, Betty told women from all over the world that they would have to fight for their own equality. She also warned that "forces that control the governments of the U.N. might try to use International Woman's Year to...control the women's movement."

Betty's warning was already evident in the official speeches in

100

Mexico City. Delegates from each country—many were wives of national leaders—rose to explain how well off women were in their own nations. Many of the women from the Third World countries of Africa, South America, and the Middle East linked women's rights to economic changes or political changes. Jehan Sadat, wife of the president of Egypt, insisted that women's liberation had to be linked to the rights of Palestinians, who were fighting against Israel.

When Leah Rabin, wife of the prime minister of Israel, rose to speak, all the delegates from the Communist, Arab, and some African and Asian countries walked out. Leah Rabin ignored this massive gesture and continued speaking, but Betty was shocked.

She was sure that outside forces were trying to prevent the unofficial delegates from meeting. Betty was followed, and questioned by the attorney general of Mexico. He worried that the nongovernmental women delegates were planning a protest march.

Many of the Americans returned home deeply disappointed with this international conference of women. For the first time, they realized that their personal goals presented a real threat to other forces, both in America and in the world.

And back in the United States, committed feminists had to face the possibility that ERA would fail; that indeed, the fight for equality was far from over.

Opposition to ERA and all other feminist goals had been quietly building in the United States. Immediately after Congress passed ERA, opposition to it became stronger and better organized. The women's movement, already counting on victory, had failed to understand this until much later. It needed to organize and fight for state by state passage of the amendment.

Throughout the 1970s Betty spoke out for ERA wherever she went. In 1976 she returned to Peoria to build support for it.

By then, social change was evident, even in conservative Peoria. A NOW chapter had been formed, and an active group of women was ready to lobby in the state capital to help pass ERA. Together with hundreds of other Peoria women, Betty boarded a bus for the capital, Springfield, to rally for the amendment.

In spite of her efforts and those of many other women, by 1978 Betty's home state of Illinois had twice defeated ERA in its state legislature.

It became clear that the Equal Rights Amendment was in trouble. Again, Betty took time out from her busy schedule of writing and teaching to campaign for the amendment. She understood clearly that there were only a few months left before the deadline for ratification. Illinois' defeat almost certainly "doomed the constitutional underpinning of women's rights for this century."

With another reunion of Betty's high school class scheduled for June 1978, Betty returned once again to Peoria. Her high school reunion of 1963 had been very disappointing. She did not look forward to returning. However, ERA was too important.

Despite ERA's failure in its state, Peoria's NOW chapter was not ready to give up. "If you come home, we will have a march in Peoria, and the women will take heart again," NOW leader Ann Courtney told Betty.

Putting aside her fear of another rejection at the reunion, Betty came. With an invitation to stay at the home of Harriet Parkhurst, one of her oldest friends, Betty trusted that this time things would be different. And they were.

The torchlight parade to Peoria's courthouse was more successful than anyone had hoped. There were about 1,000 women, men, and children who came out to march in support of equal rights for women. When Betty got up to speak, they applauded enthusiastically. "Tonight in Peoria," Betty proclaimed, "we can see that the majority of women don't want to go back, and the men don't want them to go back."

Later that week, at the fortieth reunion of the class of 1938, Betty felt more welcome too. Everyone seemed glad to see her. Alone, without Carl or the children, Betty was mellower and more confident.

A few months later, in an article she wrote in *The New York Times* about her visit, Betty admitted: "I remembered only the pain of growing up in Peoria. I never would admit the sweet sure certainty of belonging..."

At this reunion, forty years after she first left Peoria, Betty had finally recaptured the good times and the positive experiences that had been her roots. She rebuilt the bridges between herself and her family and friends. Betty began to see that much more than women's rights had changed in Peoria.

Betty sat with her brother, Harry, and the Parkhursts on the

On the fortieth anniversary of her graduation from Whittier Grade School, Betty posed for a photo with her classmates. (She is third from right in the second row.)

beautiful terrace of the exclusive country club. Her parents had once been excluded from membership here because they were Jews. She had suffered from that exclusion back in high school. Now it was just a memory.

Harriet, "Parky," Bob, and all her other non-Jewish friends might shrug it all off as having little importance. Even her brother denied the seriousness of his own experiences, insisting that sororities and fraternities were not important. For Betty, the feeling of unfairness had been stronger and more insistent. She now understood that her childhood— what she had learned about justice, plus her own feelings of injustice—had led her "to the women's movement in the world."

Betty left Peoria with more positive feelings than when she had come. She carried those feelings with her to Washington, D.C. where, on July 9, a national march for ERA was planned.

NOW had organized this march to rally for an extension for the amendment. The original seven-year time limit was running out. Thirty-five states had already ratified ERA. Only three more were needed. The women's movement felt sure it could get ERA passed if only there was a bit more time.

The 1978 march on Washington was a huge success in terms of numbers. Women came from all over the country. They arrived singly and in groups, by plane, train, and bus. All the women were dressed in white, in imitation of a similar march fifty years before. Then women had rallied in Washington to fight for the right to vote.

Betty was no longer active in NOW and was not involved in major planning for the march. However, she did arrange to visit Illinois Congressmen to urge them to vote for the extension of the ERA deadline. While on Capitol Hill, Betty met Kathy Railsback, the daughter of Congressman Tom Railsback of Illinois.

"What can I do to help?" asked Kathy, who later called Betty at her hotel.

Betty, always the organizer, wasted no time in giving Kathy a job. Together with Betty's niece, Laurie, Kathy organized the sons and daughters of Congress "to demand that their dads pass the Equal Rights Amendment."

The ERA extension was passed by Congress, giving women a little more than three years — thirty-nine months — to get the extra states to ratify the amendment. Although a small victory, it was a second chance. It also gave a boost to the belief that reforming the system, rather than changing it, was the answer.

Leaving one of her many meetings at the White House, Betty paused for a photo.

Ms. Magazine and the women involved in NOW and the political caucus led a boycott against any state that had not yet ratified ERA. They wanted to show that women had the power and the ability to do economic harm to states that did not support equal rights for women. If women refused to buy products made in those states, and refused to hold conferences there, they might be able to force a change in policy. Betty was not so sure that this strategy always worked.

The Central Conference of American Rabbis had planned its next nationwide meeting in 1979 in Arizona, a state that had not ratified ERA. Should the handful of women who had recently become rabbis boycott and refuse to go?

When Laura Geller, a young woman rabbi, called to ask her opinion, Betty's advice was: "Go, and bring someone to focus the issue of the convention on feminism."

Rabbi Laura Geller not only took Betty's advice but Betty was invited to come and speak to the women. Many male rabbis also came to hear her. Since then Laura Geller has been a friend and supporter of Betty Friedan.

Other women continued to accuse Betty of betraying the movement. "I don't want to ignore her role in beginning the whole thing with her book," said one well-known feminist. But, she claimed, she has done so much harm to the movement that it has negated her early accomplishments.

Other women charged that Betty Friedan was a "narrowly focused reformer" whose ideas about liberation did not extend beyond "educated white women."

Betty had not planned to write another book on women or the women's movement. For some time, she had been concentrating on her work about aging. As Betty approached her sixtieth year, this subject was of increasing interest to her.

It was while teaching at various colleges and meeting the new generation of women that Betty began to believe what she had suspected since 1970. The women's movement had gotten off the track. A false and unnecessary division had been created between feminism and the family. This division, she felt, was endangering all the gains that women had won. Betty put aside the book on aging to express these ideas in *The Second Stage*.

When Betty's third book *The Second Stage*, was published in 1981, feminist leaders and followers were almost unanimous in their anger at its author. *The Second Stage* drew a tirade of criticism. Betty was accused of denying all that women had fought for during the past twenty years.

Not so, insisted Betty, who claimed the message of her book had been distorted. "There is not the slightest sense of my turning back on anything of the women's movement," she said. "In fact, every word I say in *The Second Stage* indicates how important I think the women's movement has been for women."

The Second Stage, like *The Feminine Mystique*, was ahead of its time. Hopeful and optimistic as ever, Betty had concentrated mainly on the gains that feminism had made instead of highlighting what was still left to accomplish. She also pointed out what she considered the mistakes of the women's movement.

As Betty explained, something was "going wrong" in the way women were "trying to live the equality we fought for." Women had "overreacted," she said, "mimicking men" and "denying their human needs for love and intimacy."

Betty told women that they must work together with men in this "second stage" of the revolution. She had several suggestions for doing this, such as a change in working hours so that men and women could share in child care. As always, she reminded women: "men are not the enemy." We need men, she wrote, to help us to improve society.

Despite continued opposition, even fury, over her latest book, Betty remained a celebrity. With three published books, and scores of articles and interviews, she was considered an expert on women in society. If the women's movement had turned its back on her, the mainstream now began to accept Betty Friedan. One year after the book was written, Betty was chosen as author of the year by the American Society of Journalists and Authors.

Toward the end of the 1970s, departments of women's studies were becoming part of many college campuses. Serious scholars expanded their ideas to include an interest in women. Sociology, political science, history, psychology, and literature all began to be examined from women's points of view. There was an explosion of books about women.

Betty had been guest lecturer at many universities since 1970. In 1979 she became a Senior Research Associate at the Center for Social Sciences at Columbia University, in New York City, where she taught for three years. After the bitter criticism of her and her book, she retreated even more from the organized women's movement.

"I was much better off once I simply kept to my own role that nobody could take away from me, of writing and speaking..." Betty finally realized. "I was very good at the vision and at inspiring...and at organizing...I was not good at fighting defensive battles where I simply tried to hold on to my own power."

12

Making New History

After three years at Columbia University, Betty went on to Cambridge, Massachusetts. Here, she was first a fellow at the Institute of Politics, Harvard University John F. Kennedy School of Government, and then a joint fellow at Harvard's Center for Population Studies.

It was in 1982, while she was living in Cambridge, that ERA failed. The three-year extension had expired without getting the ratification of thirty-eight of the fifty states.

Betty reminisced with a Boston *Globe* reporter about her reactions to this disappointment for the cause of women's rights.

"It never occurred to women that they wouldn't get the equal rights amendment," she explained. Betty felt that the defeat of ERA was a "blot on America." But still the optimist, she added: "a miracle did happen in the battle. The political power of women became organized and...that is going to absolutely change...the politics of America."

Sitting in her penthouse apartment on the top floor of a Harvard dormitory building, she admitted that feminist anger at her book *The Second Stage* had caused her considerable pain. "It was as if people criticized it without even reading it," she said.

A few writers would claim that *The Second Stage* had reinforced the backlash against feminism, which helped defeat ERA. Betty herself did not believe that.

Perhaps one of the best things that happened to Betty during the 1970s was her growing satisfaction in her family. Her three children were successful adults with careers of their own. Jonathan and Emily were both married.

Betty became a grandmother when Jonathan and his wife Helen had a son. "It is very satisfying to be Raphael Friedan's grandmother," Betty told a reporter. She described her grandson as "a loving, marvelous bundle of life."

Betty Friedan was also full of life. She was active and busier than ever. "I feel on the move again," she told a reporter before she left Cambridge in 1982.

At sixty-one, Betty was involved with work on her latest book *The Fountain of Age*. The tables in her New York apartment and her weekend home on Long Island were stacked high with notes and papers, interviews, and statistics. Alan Walker, her agent since 1971, had no trouble booking her for speeches at several thousand dollars plus expenses for each appearance.

Less than ten years before, Betty had written in her diary that her need for fame was caused by her deep feelings that she was "no good as an ordinary woman." In the 1970s those feelings had affected many aspects of her life. Her relationships with others were stormy, her appearance seemed unkempt, her speeches were rambling and sometimes confused. In the 1980s things began to change for the better. Betty was challenging herself with "new questions, new pursuits, new goals, new purposes...a new beginning."

Betty had a long list of accomplishments behind her. She was a principal founder of NOW and the National Women's Political Caucus and an author of three important books. She was a visiting professor at leading universities, an organizer and director of the First Women's Bank in New York City. The Girl Scouts of America gave her their

Humanist of the Year award in 1975, and she was an Author of the Year in 1982.

Her commitment to justice was still the driving force behind many of Betty's activities. She traveled to Cambridge University, in England, in 1983 to debate the statement: *Feminism Is Good for Men.*

In 1984 Betty again had the opportunity to travel to Israel. She was invited to give one of two opening addresses to a major women's meeting in Jerusalem. This conference, organized and sponsored by the American Jewish Congress, was called Woman as Jew, Jew as

Betty became a veteran traveler, making speeches about women all over the world. Here, she takes time out for shopping.

Woman: An Urgent Inquiry. Its purpose was to examine the unique problems that women had, both in Jewish society and in the Jewish religion.

Facing a large crowd of women and some men, Betty spoke about recent history, the history she herself had made. She told the audience what it was like for women in America back in the 1950s and '60s. She explained how women had changed things by applying the principles of American democracy to their own lives. Then she discussed her impressions of Israel and some of the changes she had seen for women since her first visit in 1972.

Betty's keynote speech was just the beginning of a conference of lectures, meetings, and discussions. At the end of four days of sessions, another American feminist, Anne Roiphe, remembered that it was Betty's "brilliant" suggestion for all the participants to march to the King David Hotel. More than 100 women assembled in front of the Van Leer Institute, where the conference was held. They walked the six blocks to the King David, the well-known hotel where Israel's newly elected leaders were holding talks.

The marchers chanted in Hebrew: "No government on women's backs." They wanted to urge government officials to ignore party lines when considering Israeli women's need for "equality and simple justice."

"For most of the Israelis this was their first feminist action," Anne Roiphe recalled. "To be a part of such a moment makes one giddy with hope. We hugged each other, we exchanged addresses." There were cheers when the message came from the two leaders, Shimon Peres and Yitzhak Shamir, that they would meet with a delegation of the women.

Although smaller in scope, this woman's march in Jerusalem was not unlike the American march for equality. Fourteen years earlier, that march had passed through the streets of New York instead of Jerusalem. Betty had led both. And this time too, it had been her idea that had set it in motion.

Two important results came from this conference. One was the formation of the Israel Women's Lobby. The other was the organization of the National Commission for Women's Equality in America. This latter group was part of the American Jewish Congress. It was co-chaired by Betty Friedan and Leona Chanin.

Each year something else came up to claim Betty's time. In 1985, Betty headed the unofficial NOW delegation to the U.N. Conference for Women to be held in Nairobi, Kenya. It was the third and final conference marking the U.N. Decade of Women. This time, careful planning by American women's groups was successful. There were few signs of anti-Semitism or anti-Americanism. The tone was more peaceful and self-assured than either the Mexico City or Copenhagen conferences in 1975 and 1980. Most of the delegates were independent women committed to feminist goals. They were not just the wives of political leaders who had been sent by their governments.

Betty returned from Nairobi with good feelings about the direction of feminism. In her speeches she said: "Deliver us to the new problems. They are more interesting than the old ones." She meant that the reality of women's lives in America was different than it had been.

Twenty years ago, explains Betty, women had to deal with the problems of returning to work or school, struggling with the guilt of leaving their children in someone else's care. Today, so many women are working, Betty says. The problems now involve questions such as how husbands and wives will share the housework or finding the best day care for the children.

"We've really broken through the feminine mystique. I mean, women are people," Betty told a *Newsday* reporter. "We define ourselves as people, we're seen as people. It's just taken for granted by the new generation of women."

With her impatience and her brusque manner, Betty had made many enemies. However, when she wanted to organize something new, nothing could stop her. In 1986, at the forty-eighth international conference of PEN (an association of writers) Betty formed a separate women's committee. At her home in Sag Harbor, she started a group called the Sag Harbor Initiative, made up of prominent members of that community, to discuss current political and social issues.

In her personal life, Betty seemed more relaxed to her friends and associates.

Betty's agent, Alan Walker, admitted that although Betty is demanding and short tempered, she "has mellowed over the years and is much more relaxed."

Betty's brother, Harry, a successful businessman and community leader in Peoria, agreed. Closer to his sister than he once was, Harry insisted that Betty didn't mean to be rude. She was simply impatient. "Today, I find her the mellowest I can recall," Harry said.

Harriet Vance Parkhurst did not remember Betty ever being rude or irritable when she was young. She found it surprising when she first noticed how "short" she was with other people. More recently, however, Betty is warm and friendly. She jokes that her old friend "Parky" is "her favorite male chauvinist pig."

"She has a great quality about her," says Harriet Parkhurst. Explaining how Betty has managed to keep in touch with her old classmates, Harriet explains: "She has staying power."

That "staying power" kept Betty close to the friends in her extended family commune too. Although their first rented beach house in the Hamptons was given up long ago, Betty still considers that group of friends to be special.

One of her friends described her home in Sag Harbor as "a two-story frame house with a deck overlooking the cove. There is a wonderful kitchen with a lot of light," and enough bedrooms to accommodate the members of her "family of friends" whenever they visit. The group still gets together for Thanksgiving and other family-oriented holidays. They have never stopped feeling close to one another. And of course, Betty's children and grandchildren continue to visit her there too.

In 1985, Betty accepted an invitation to be a joint visiting professor at the University of Southern California School of Journalism and Women's Studies. She teaches at the university from January to May and continues her research in gerontology, the study of aging. And now "my asthma has stopped since I am no longer here in New York in the cold months," explains Betty.

This assignment has expanded Betty's life a great deal. She has met new friends of all ages and continues growing and learning.

One of her younger friends is Rabbi Laura Geller, who first consulted her about the conference of American rabbis in 1979. Rabbi Geller is the executive director of Hillel, the Jewish student group on campus. She runs a Jewish study group in which Betty Friedan is a "wonderful participant," learning more about her own Jewish heritage, ritual, and tradition.

Also in California, Betty created a think tank, a project of the Institute of Women and Men in Society at the University of Southern California. The group includes a variety of different people in business, politics, the media, and the university. They meet once a month and then have a day-long retreat at which they discuss such topics as Beyond the Male Model as applied to housing, education, the arts, power, and work.

When Betty Friedan's mother, Miriam, died late in the spring of 1988, Betty was still in California. It was to her friends here that she turned after coming back from the funeral service in Peoria. Needing something of her own to mark her mother's death, Betty arranged an informal memorial service at her home in Santa Monica.

At the service, Betty spoke about her mother, recalling how strong she was. She related her accomplishments, her energy, and her ability to live a creative life until she died at the age of ninety. Then her friends spoke of their feelings about their own mothers.

Over the years, Betty Friedan had written of her mother's faults both privately and publicly, insisting that "she was never a role model for me." With her mother no longer alive, Betty perhaps has attempted to make peace with her feelings and her memories.

Betty Naomi Goldstein Friedan is still fighting — for what she believes and for what she wants. She continues to build a life of accomplishment based on her own talents and experiences, her "personal truth" as she calls it. Betty's book on aging promises to be another ground-breaking work. And Betty, a pioneer again in her later years, is asserting that "old age is a new period for human growth."

While writing her book on aging, Betty continues to work with women of all ages. Here she meets with women at Smith College.

The girl who thought her mother was unhappy and unfulfilled without "real" work found work that she loved.

The girl who organized clubs in elementary school went on to form NOW and to rally women all over the world.

The girl who loved to dress up and to act in plays now lectures to students, women's groups, and corporations.

The girl who wrote for the school newspaper and founded literary magazines went on to write important books and hundreds of columns and articles.

The girl who was a high school valedictorian and who graduated from Smith College *summa cum laude* developed a scholarly career as visiting professor at major universities.

The girl who longed for "someone to love her, and work that was important" certainly found her important work. She has not found someone who would "love her best," but neither has she given up. She is still hoping for "companionship and intimacy."

Betty does not like to look back. Whatever she has done was right for its time. She will not dwell on errors or mistakes.

The mention of Betty Friedan's name still "sends some people through the roof." But perhaps Betty has learned to live with and accept herself. She has often quoted one of her favorite heroines, Joan of Arc, saying: "All that I am I will not deny."

Afterword

What is Betty Friedan really like? After reading thousands of words by and about her, watching her at work, and speaking with her privately we realize there is no simple answer to that question.

Betty Friedan has often been written about negatively by the very reporters and journalists to whom she reluctantly, grudgingly gave time. Although her telephone numbers and addresses are public, she is nevertheless not very accessible.

"I'm too busy to speak with you now," are almost the first words she utters when she picks up her telephone. Returning a call from an associate, she snaps: "This is Betty. What do you want?" She takes small favors for granted; rarely says "thank you" and is too pressed for "hello" or "good-bye." However, she is quick to apologize for her brusqueness or her irritability, blaming it on the pressures of work.

Betty's apartment has a large picture window with a view of New York City's Lincoln Center for the Performing Arts and beyond it, the Hudson River. Her living room, decorated in warm reds — one of Betty's favorite colors — is lined with books. In one corner, the old Victorian love seat, which she purchased at an auction in Rockland

County, is a reminder of other times. The room is accented with small tables, lamps, and other pieces brought back from her many travels.

"Have you seen this?" she asked us, pointing to a child's composition. The piece, written by her daughter, Emily, is framed and hangs on the wall of her study alcove. The three lines, carefully printed in neat letters, inform us that Emily once wanted to be an author like her mother.

Above the frame, on a shelf, sits a large color photo of the Friedan family. Betty casually gestures in that direction to show us her grown children, their spouses and the grandchildren. She has allowed us to follow her around, and this is the end of the day. We watched Betty Friedan taping a local television program, moderated by an old friend. Then we listened to her speak before a group of experts on aging, in a seminar sponsored jointly by American and Japanese groups.

The speech brought her a standing ovation. In this, her newest area of research, she has again managed to turn all the old rules around. Betty is now questioning everyone's assumptions about aging, just as she once questioned their assumptions about women.

Twenty-five years before, Betty Friedan said: "Women are people." Today, no one doubts it. And now again she is explaining that when you get older, you still need the same things: work and love. You need a family, and if you don't have a blood family, you can create a family of friends, just as she did.

In spite of the assurance of continuous applause, she asked us: "Well, how was it?" "Wonderful," we answered sincerely.

A few weeks later, on a bitter cold day in January, Betty Friedan arrives at a TV station for yet another taping. She will be leaving for the University of Southern California in four days and is looking forward to warmer weather.

Betty arrives late, dressed in a red sweater and matching red shoes. With her is Anne Summers, the new editor of *Ms.* Magazine, who will be interviewed with her. Proudly, Betty shows us the latest issue of *Ms.*, which includes an article about her.

"This is the first time I've ever been in *Ms.*," Betty explains to us. "Because Gloria Steinem (the previous editor) and I...Well, you know..." Betty's voice trails off and we nod. We know about her differences with Gloria Steinem.

Betty Friedan and Anne Summers are steered in to be made up before the show. "I need all the help you can give me," Betty says, smiling. She reappears shortly after, her hair recombed softly and with some red lipstick that picks up the color of her sweater.

"How do you want to be referred to on the TV credits?" the producer asks. Betty thinks a minute. "As the author of *The Feminine Mystique* and *The Second Stage*." She has too many other credentials to list them all underneath her picture.

The show begins and we watch on the monitor in the studio. The interviewer introduces her as the person who wrote: "Women need to develop and grow like men."

Betty Friedan cups her chin in her hand, a gesture now very familiar to us. She has heard all of this too many times to count. The questions hardly challenge her.

In her earliest television appearances, Betty was known to have shouted above the critical voice of the interviewer and to have interrupted other guests to make her points. Today her ideas are mainstream. Betty is relaxed and pleasant.

"Women start today from a place they wouldn't have dreamed of twenty-five years ago. They see the possibilities open to them and the assumptions of equality," Betty explains.

Betty still speaks rapidly, in her distinctive, husky voice. "Women have achieved enough to be leading completely different lives. The second stage does have new problems, but they are so much more interesting than the old ones. Women *do* have choices."

Betty's own daughter is a doctor. Her daughter-in-law, Helen, the mother of two children, is studying to be a rabbi.

"Women have important choices to make," affirms Betty. But the interviewer prods her. There is still not equity in pay or in child care.

There is "unfinished business," Betty concedes. But these twenty-five years (since *The Feminine Mystique* was written) have seen the first woman — Sandra Day O'Connor — appointed to the Supreme Court of the United States, and two women — astronaut Judith Resnick and schoolteacher Christa McAuliffe — die in space. "Today, the problem is choice," Betty repeats. "The world is open to young women."

All these successes and changes, a veritable revolution, were brought about by groups of women, many of them unknown, who steadily worked in their own communities. No one could have done it alone. However, Betty Friedan is perhaps the single most important person responsible for the changes and the choices in women's lives today.

At a symposium on aging, Betty chats with the authors.

Although no longer actively involved in the organized women's movement, she is the one who is called upon for her opinion when an issue in the news relates to women. It is her name that is recognized around the world as a leader and founder of the women's movement.

Her life today involves writing, teaching, and lecturing. Spending time with friends, Betty says, is her way to relax, and she has many friends all over the world.

Betty Friedan would like women to have work that matters to them, just as she has. And she wants them to have all the choices that men have.

Back in her own apartment, struggling with her answering machine, sitting in the dark because she forgot to buy a bulb for the light over her desk, Betty scribbles her messages. She has said: "I work as much as a Senator with a staff of fifty, and I don't even have a full-time secretary!"

We know she works hard. We sympathize with the pressures as Betty barks into her telephone, setting up appointments, giving instructions, making demands. We remind her of what she herself has said: "All any person needs to be happy is work and love."

Betty answers softly: "But when you love your work, you have everything."

Chronology

1920 — Harry Goldstein and Miriam Horwitz marry.

1921 — Betty Naomi Goldstein is born to Miriam Horwitz Goldstein and Harry Goldstein in Peoria, Illinois on February 4.

1938 — Betty graduates from Central High School in June, one of five valedictorians.

1942 — Betty graduates with honors from Smith College in June. Betty becomes a graduate student in psychology at the University of California at Berkeley.

1943 — Harry Goldstein, Betty's father, dies.
Despite receiving a fellowship for further study, Betty leaves Berkeley, moves to New York City, and works as a reporter.

1947 — Betty and Carl Friedan are married by a Justice of the Peace in June.

1948 — Daniel Friedan is born in October.

1952 — Jonathan Friedan is born in November.

1956 — Emily Friedan is born in May.

1957 — Betty is asked to prepare a questionnaire for her fifteenth reunion of Smith College. This is the basis of the research that becomes her first book.

1963 — *The Feminine Mystique* is completed after five years of research and published by W.W. Norton & Co.

1964 — Betty edits the June issue of the women's magazine *Ladies' Home Journal*.

1966 — National Organization for Women (NOW) is founded with Betty Friedan as its president.

NOW's second annual convention is held. Betty Friedan presents the Bill of Rights for women.

1969 — NOW organizes a sit-in at the Oak Room of the Plaza Hotel in New York City.

Betty and Carl Friedan are divorced in May.

1970 — Betty testifies before a congressional committee against President Richard Nixon's nomination of G. Harrold Carswell to the Supreme Court.

Betty steps down as president of NOW and is succeeded by Aileen Hernandez.

Betty organizes the Women's Strike for Equality, including a march down Fifth Avenue in New York City. It takes place on August 26. Over 50,000 women participate.

In a clash with the newly formed Women's Strike Coalition, Betty resigns from that group after the second march in December.

1970 – — Betty is a lecturer and a scholar in residence at major
1979 universities in the United States.

1971 — On February 4, Betty reaches her fiftieth birthday while traveling in England.

National Women's Political Caucus is founded by Bella Abzug, Gloria Steinem, and Betty Friedan.

1972 — Betty's first visit to Israel.

Betty is elected as a delegate to the 1972 Democratic Convention in Miami, Florida.

1973 — Betty Friedan receives an audience with Pope Paul in Rome.

1974 — Betty travels to Iran at the invitation of the Women's Organization of Iran, and meets the Shah.

1975 — Betty receives an honorary degree from her alma mater, Smith College.

At the first conference of the U.N. Decade of Women, in Mexico City, Betty is invited to speak to the Tribune of nongovernmental organizations.

1976 — *It Changed My Life*, Betty's second book, is published.

1978 — The March on Washington, organized by NOW, draws 100,000 marchers to urge an extension of time for the passage of ERA.

1980 — The second conference marking the U.N. Decade of Women is held in Copenhagen.

1981 — *The Second Stage*, Betty's third book, is published and meets a barrage of criticism.

1982 — Betty is invited to lecture at Harvard University.

1985 — Betty heads the unofficial NOW delegation to the final U.N. conference in Nairobi, Kenya.

She accepts an invitation to be a joint visiting professor at the University of Southern California.

1988 — Miriam Horwitz Goldstein, Betty's mother, dies at the age of ninety.

1989 — *The Fountain of Age*, Betty's fourth book, is nearing completion. She continues writing, teaching, and lecturing.

INDEX